More Math Logic Mysteries

Mathematical Problem Solving With Deductive Reasoning

Marilynn L. Rapp Buxton

Illustrated by David Parker

PRUFROCK PRESS INC.

Prufrock Press Inc.
P.O. Box 8813
Waco, TX 76714-8813
Phone: (800) 998-2208
Fax: (800) 240-0333
http://www.prufrock.com

Contents

Easy Puzzles

Medium Puzzles

Difficult Puzzles

Formidable Puzzles

Teacher's Guide

College professors and business professionals have told me, "Teach kids to work hard and how to think." I teach elementary gifted and talented students, as well as other classes, creative thinking (fluency, flexibility, originality, elaboration, and problem solving), and critical thinking (labeling, observation, analogies, classification, webbing, comparison, patterning, sequencing, syllogisms, cause and effect, table logic, and matrix logic). Most students enjoy matrix puzzles enough to ask for more!

But, how can a teacher justify "puzzle time" when there are standards to meet and no child to leave behind? What about students who finish assignments (especially math) and ask, "What should I do now?" What if you had a math matrix book?

This book is unique in that it contains challenging vocabulary and requires students to use logical reasoning and perform a variety of operations and skills that align with state and national standards (fractions, decimals, exponents, place value, sequencing, patterning, algebra, time, probability, percent, measurement, number line, area, volume, weight, and temperature). Students will make hypotheses, draw conclusions, organize information, and use syllogistic thinking. Teachers can feel confident they are providing rigor and reinforcing required skills in a format that students enjoy.

My students helped ensure that this book is kid-friendly and puzzles can be solved by kids. The Table of Contents ranks puzzles from easy to challenging and identifies the emphasized required skills.

Students should be able to work independently if they heed instructions and refer to the solutions for step-by-step explanation of reasoning. Teachers and parents may use the solutions as an answer key or allow students to self-check and clarify their work. Giving students the sample problem and information for working matrix puzzles (see pp. 6–8) is a good way to refresh students' memories of how logic puzzles work or to introduce the beginning matrix solver to the steps he or she should take to finish the problem.

This book may be used for alternate work during compacting, enrichment, centers, or just for fun. Students may work alone, with a partner, in a group, or whatever suits the needs of the teacher and students. A student who fully understands the reasoning of a particular puzzle could demonstrate it to the class. You also can use this book in combination with its companion book, *Math Logic Mysteries*, to introduce students to countless math logic puzzles on multiple challenge levels.

I hope this book will be a helpful resource for teachers who strive to provide challenging and applicable math enrichment that is enjoyable for students who love to think!

—Marilynn

How to Do Matrix Puzzles

Matrix puzzles are fun, and they are good exercise for your brain. They help you develop good critical and logical thinking skills. In this book, you have the extra challenge of performing a math operation or calculation during each puzzle.

Always read the puzzle introductions. They explain the situation and contain essential information. For example, a clue might say, "Chris likes hamburgers, and all of the girls like pizza." Is Chris a girl or boy? The introduction said: "Two brothers (Chris and Eric) have a sister named Kylene." Add that with the clue and deduce that Chris is a boy, so he doesn't eat pizza. You would not be able to solve the puzzle without that information.

After you read the introduction, begin reading clues. If you discover a "no" clue, mark an × in the box where two items meet. Sometimes you can mark several boxes. For example, "A girl likes peanut butter." Mark × for all boys, but you don't know which girl likes it, so leave the girl boxes blank. If you discover a "yes" clue, mark O in the box. When you mark O, also mark × in the boxes above, beneath, and beside the O.

After you have read all of the clues and marked the boxes, look up and down and across to see if any columns or rows have only one box left. That will be a "yes," or O. There should be one O in every column and every row of a section. Try the sample below and read the solution.

Sample Matrix Puzzle

Four friends went shopping for school supplies. Each student purchased two different items, and nobody bought the same number of items. Read the clues and discover how many items each student bought.

	1	2	3	4	5	6	7	8
Claude								
Harry								
Nan								
Tom								
5				
6				
7				
8				

Clues

1. Neither Tom nor the student who got five highlighters chose four erasers.
2. Neither Claude nor the student who purchased two notebooks bought six folders.
3. Neither Nan nor the student who bought eight markers selected three packages of paper or four erasers.
4. Neither Tom nor the student who got two notebooks purchased five highlighters or seven pencils.

Solution:

- Clue 1 tells us that Tom isn't 5 or 4, and 5 doesn't go with 4. Mark an × at the intersection of Tom and 4, Tom and 5, and 4 and 5.

- Clue 2 tells us that Claude isn't 2 or 6, and 2 doesn't go with 6. Mark an × at the intersection of Claude and 2, Claude and 6, and 2 and 6.

- Clue 3 tells us that Nan isn't 8, 3, or 4, and 8 doesn't go with 3 or 4. Mark an × at the intersection of Nan and 8, Nan and 3, Nan and 4, 8 and 3, and 8 and 4.

- Clue 4 tells us that Tom isn't 2, 5, or 7, and 2 doesn't go with 5 or 7. Mark an × at the intersection of Tom and 2 (Tom and 5 is already marked × from Clue 1), Tom and 7, 2 and 5, and 2 and 7. So, 2 goes with 8 (only one left). Mark an O at the intersection of 2 and 8 and an × at the intersection of 1 and 8.

Answers: After further deduction, you find that Claude is 4 and 7, Harry is 2 and 8, Nan is 1 and 5, and Tom is 3 and 6.

Hints for Solving Matrix Puzzles

Some puzzles contain three or more sections such as first name, last name, and someone's favorite hobby. Be careful to mark only one section of the matrix. Sometimes you know first and last name, first name and hobby, or last name and hobby. Transfer information from one section to another using syllogistic thinking. A syllogism says, "Apples are fruit. Fruit is good to eat. Therefore, apples are good to eat." Use syllogistic thinking on this clue:

Anne likes purple. The girl who likes purple sings well. Therefore, _____ sings well.

You would mark Anne with purple, purple with sings well, and Anne with sings well.

Carefully read clues to get correct and complete information. Here are a few other examples:

1. If a clue says, "Neither Tara nor the banker drove a car," that means three things: Tara didn't drive a car, the banker didn't drive a car, and Tara is not the banker.

2. A clue such as "The three girls are Mindy, the one wearing the red sweater, and the one whose birthday is in July" indicates three different people. Mindy doesn't wear the red sweater and her birthday is not in July. The one wearing a red sweater does not have a birthday in July.

3. Combine information from clues. Look for the same topic in several clues. Clue 1 says, "Lynn's last name is Brown." Clue 3 says, "Mrs. Brown rides a motorcycle." Clue 5 says, "Lynn is a teacher." Combine the clues about Lynn and Brown to find that Lynn Brown is a teacher who rides a motorcycle.

Solutions for Matrix Puzzles

Solutions for each of the puzzles can be found in the back of the book. Use the descriptions to help you if you get stuck on a puzzle. Your teacher may use the solutions to check your accuracy or you may self-check your own answers.

Name: Date:

Let's Play Ball

Five cousins (four girls and a boy named LeRoy) play ball games every recess at school. They tally their points each week. During the last 2 weeks, one player dominated nearly every game and ended up winning the September points award. Convert fractions to decimals, and then multiply to determine the correct score for each player. For example: ½ of 54 is .5 × 54 = 27. Round decimals to the nearest whole number. For example:

- ⅑ is the decimal .111 . . . , so ⅑ of 36 is .111 × 36 = 3.996. Round to 4.
- ⅔ is the decimal .666 . . . , so ⅔ of 24 is .666 × 24 = 15.984. Round to 16.

Clues

1. One child earned ½ as many points as JoAnn.
2. LaVonne's total was ⅔ of Ann's score.
3. LaVonne scored ½ as many points as LeRoy.
4. LeRoy tallied ⁸⁄₉ as many points as Louise.

	24	36	48	54	72
Ann					
JoAnn					
LaVonne					
LeRoy					
Louise					

Happy Birth Date to You

Seven kids live on the same street. Their parents traditionally have a block party to celebrate their birthdays together. They were all born in February, but on different days. Read the clues and use your knowledge of fractions to determine the correct birth date for each child.

Clues

1. Grant's birth date is ½ of Lars' date.
2. Lars' birth date is ⅔ of Valerie's date.
3. Onalee's birth date is ⅓ of Trey's date.
4. Emilio's birth date is ¼ of Grant's date.

	Feb. 2	Feb. 4	Feb. 8	Feb. 10	Feb. 12	Feb. 16	Feb. 24
Bruce							
Emilio							
Grant							
Lars							
Onalee							
Trey							
Valerie							

I'll Be a Bunny for Money

Six pals challenged each other to a "Bunny Hop" contest. Each put in $2 for the winner's pot. From the starting line, contestants hopped with their feet together as far as possible until they quit, got tired, their feet came apart, or they fell over! Distances were marked, and the winner took home $12. Calculate the percentages and match each pal with the distance he or she hopped. You will need to round to the nearest hundredths place. *Note*: Hopping 25% farther than 60 meters means 25% of 60 (.25 × 60) = 15 m more than 60, or 15 m + 60 m = 75 m. Or, you can multiply 60 × 1.25 (100% + 25%) = 75 m. Hopping 55% less than 60 meters means 55% of 60 (.55 × 60) = 33 m less than 60, or 60 m − 33 m = 27 m. Or, you can multiply 60 × .45 (100% − 55%) = 27 m.

Clues

1. Waverly hopped about 78% farther than another child.
2. Pearl got the giggles and fell over while laughing. She hopped 39% less than someone.
3. Razi ended up hopping 13% less than the one who hopped 64% farther than Pearl.
4. Somebody hopped about 9% less than Kaiya.
5. Dale hopped about 12% farther than one friend.

	86.1 meters	122.84 meters	141.2 meters	155.25 meters	218.66 meters	245 meters
Dale						
Kaiya						
Langley						
Pearl						
Razi						
Waverly						

They Got Speed

Nine students on a class trip huddled around their motel window watching interstate traffic when they decided to challenge one another to guess the speed of particular vehicles passing by. One would call out "red van," for example, while another would guess the red van's speed. A third student verified the mph as the vehicle passed under the digital readout panel mounted on the overpass. Finish the chart by writing in the differences between the actual and guessed miles per hour. Read the clues and match each student with his or her actual and/or guessed speeds.

Clues

1. The actual speed of Walter's car was less than Diana's, whose vehicle was slower than Jade's.
2. Phyllis was 3 mph off and Daryl was 1 mph off the actual speed.
3. Karen guessed 2 mph off, Diana guessed exactly, and David guessed 1 mph off the actual.
4. Jade guessed too low, while Walter guessed correctly.
5. Karen, Daryl, and Lisa's guesses together were off a total of 6 mph too high.

mph actual ➤	55	56	58	60	61	64	65	67	68
difference ➤	+3								0
mph guess ➤	58	55	58	62	61	61	66	65	68
Daryl									
David									
Diana									
Jade									
Karen									
Lisa									
Mark									
Phyllis									
Walter									

September Sleepover

Six friends celebrated their September birthdays by having a slumber party. Their parents split the cost of three pizzas, and each girl spent less than $18 on other items. No girl bought any item that started with the same letter as her name. Calculate the cost of each item and write the sum in the "costs" row using the notes below. Then use the clues to find out how much each girl spent and which items she bought. If the pizzas cost $12 each, how could the total cost of this party be determined? What is the total cost?

$_____

Notes

- One paid for 12 apples at $0.68 each and 3 packages of cookies at $3.01 each.
- One rented 5 DVDs at $3.50 each.
- One got 12 sodas at $0.45 each, 12 bottles of water at $0.59 each, and juice for $4.99.
- One purchased veggies for $11.62 and 3 kinds of dips at $1.89 each.
- One bought decorations for $8.98, posters for $6.99, and napkins for $1.49.
- One obtained 4 bags of chips at $3.19 each and 2 flavors of salsa at $2.39 each.

Clues

1. There was a difference of less than $.20 between Bethany's and Aleasha's costs. Aleasha spent less than Bethany.
2. Chelsea, Nicole, or Vanessa spent 2% less than the girl who bought chips and salsa.
3. Neither Aleasha nor Vanessa bought beverages.
4. Bethany spent $.04 less than Dixie.
5. Nicole spent more than Chelsea but less than Dixie.

costs ➤	$	$	$	$	$	$
	apples and cookies	veggies and dips	decorations and napkins	beverages	DVD rentals	chips and salsa
Aleasha						
Bethany						
Chelsea						
Dixie						
Nicole						
Vanessa						

Newton's Newbies

Six students recently have begun attending Newton School. The counselor invited them to his office for a "get to know you" lunch. Each student told how long he or she had been at the school. Read the clues and identify which student has been at Newton for which length of time.

Clues

1. Holbrook has not been at Newton as long as Mariposa.
2. Sagar has been at Newton longer than Carlotta.
3. Mariposa has been at Newton less time than Carlotta.
4. Sagar began at Newton 2 weeks after Jamee.
5. Holbrook has been there longer than Garrison.

	1 week	2 weeks	5 weeks	6 weeks	9 weeks	11 weeks
Carlotta						
Garrison						
Holbrook						
Jamee						
Mariposa						
Sagar						

More Math Logic Mysteries © Prufrock Press Inc.
This page may be photocopied or reproduced with permission for student use.

Tri This Problem on for Size

Each Monday and Friday Mr. Whalen draws the names of four students to practice finding the area of triangles. Last week, he was elated that all four students used the formula ½(b × h) to correctly find areas. Calculate those same areas, and write the square inches in the grid. Find the decimal equivalents (numerator ÷ denominator) for the fractions in Friday's problems. Round answers to the nearest hundredths. Use the clues to find out who solved which problem on Monday and Friday.

Clues

1. Harmony calculated 68.15 sq. in. as an answer.
2. It did not take Carrington long to find 6 sq. in.
3. The student who drew 7 in. × 9 in. Monday did not get 28.69 sq. in. as an answer on Friday.
4. Wahneta figured 57.95 sq. in. on Friday, but did not calculate 8 in. × 11 in. on Monday.
5. The student who answered 39.98 sq. in. also had a triangle that was about ¼ of that area.

	Monday's Problems				Friday's Problems			
	3 in. × 4 in.	4 in. × 5 in.	7 in. × 9 in.	8 in. × 11 in.	6 ¾ in. × 8 ½ in.	7 ⅘ in. × 10 ¼ in.	9 ½ in. × 12 ⅕ in.	9 ⅖ in. × 14 ½ in.
Sq. In. ➤								
Carrington								
Harmony								
Tripp								
Wahneta								
Friday's Problems								

Piles of Pencils and Scores of Sports Cards

Six classmates were chatting on the playground about the hobbies they enjoy. Oddly, each child collects pencils and sports cards. Use the clues and do some calculating to learn who has how many pencils and how many cards.

Clues

1. Clay has 11 times more cards than Dante has pencils.
2. Oliana and the one with 24 pencils are neighbors.
3. Mamiko has ⅓ as many pencils as Clay.
4. One classmate has 12 times as many cards as pencils.
5. The one with 21 pencils has 9 times as many cards as Tanner has pencils.
6. The one with 192 cards doesn't have 13 pencils.
7. Tanner has 7 times more cards than Oliana has pencils.
8. Erika has 13 fewer cards than Dante, but twice as many pencils as Dante.

	Number of Pencils						Number of Sports Cards					
	8	13	16	21	24	32	96	117	147	176	192	205
Clay												
Dante												
Erika												
Mamiko												
Oliana												
Tanner												
Number of Sports Cards 96												
117												
147												
176												
192												
205												

More Math Logic Mysteries © Prufrock Press Inc.
This page may be photocopied or reproduced with permission for student use.

Can You Hear Me Now?

Teenagers rarely are found without their cellular phones. Three friends call each other regularly on one of their different kinds of phones. Each phone has a different weight, number of pixels for the screen, and size. Read the clues, transfer information from one section to another, and match each teen's phone with its specifications.

Clues

1. The 5.1 × 2.3 × .9 in. phone has 240 × 160 pixels.
2. The Nokia 7600 is 87 × 78 × 19 mm in size.
3. The 7 oz. phone measures 5.1 × 2.3 × .9 inches.
4. The BlackBerry's screen has 320 × 240 pixels.
5. The phone with 128 × 160 pixels weighs 123 grams.

		Size			Screen			Weight		
		5.1 × 2.3 × .9 in.	50 × 106.7 × 14.5 mm	87 × 78 × 19 mm	128 × 160 pixels	240 × 160 pixels	320 × 240 pixels	7 oz.	87.9 grams	123 grams
	BlackBerry									
	Nokia 7600									
	Sidekick 3									
Weight	7 oz.									
Weight	87.9 g									
Weight	123 g									
Screen	128 × 160									
Screen	240 × 160									
Screen	320 × 240									

Meow Mixer

Four girls all attend a cat lover's club, called "C-Club," after school. At one meeting, students compared how much food their cats ate and how much the food cost per bag. Can you use the clues to discover which cat eats which amount of food and how much it costs? Transfer information between sections.

Clues

1. Three cats are: Spencer's cat that eats ½ c. of food, Brady, and the cat that eats ⅝ c. of food.
2. Brady's and Roscoe's food does not cost $7.98 per bag.
3. The owner whose cat eats ⅝ c. of food does not pay $8.69 or $9.40 per bag.
4. Roscoe's owner is Winifred. She pays $.71 less than Jiffy's owner does for food.
5. Brady's owner pays $.71 less than the one whose cat eats ¾ c.
6. Brady eats ¼ c. more than the cat whose owner pays $10.11 per bag.

	½ cup	⅝ cup	¾ cup	⅞ cup	$7.98	$8.69	$9.40	$10.11
Brady								
Daisy								
Jiffy								
Roscoe								
$7.98								
$8.69								
$9.40								
$10.11								

American Girls

Five friends love to hang out together. They all like the colors red, white, and blue. They have unique, patriotic first names and quirky, secret nicknames for one another. One day they played a computer game at Starr's house. Use the clues to discover each girl's game score and nickname.

Clues

1. One child's name starts with the same letter as her nickname.
2. Starr earned twice as many points as the girl whose nickname is Flippy.
3. Americus scored ½ as much as Liberty.
4. Scruffy made the fewest points.
5. Independence earned ¼ as many points as Starr scored.
6. Americus' score plus Itchy's score equals Mushy's score.

	15,195	20,260	30,390	40,520	60,780	Chilly	Flippy	Itchy	Mushy	Scruffy
Americus										
Freedom										
Independence										
Liberty										
Starr										
Chilly										
Flippy										
Itchy										
Mushy										
Scruffy										

Saddle Up

Five members of the Greene County 4-H Clubs have a special adoration for horses. Leaders asked each member to share their knowledge of equine skills at a monthly club meeting. Use the clues to determine the month and topic for each member's presentation.

Clues

1. Judy gave her talk some time before Lila but after Denny. Judy's talk was not about how to bridle or saddle a horse.
2. Trudy's talk was three months before Bobby's. Neither talked about how to bridle or lead a horse.
3. The talk on shoeing a horse was two months after Denny's and one month before Lila's. Neither Denny nor Lila spoke about roping a horse.
4. The presentation about bridling a horse was one month after shoeing and one month before Bobby's, which was not about roping.

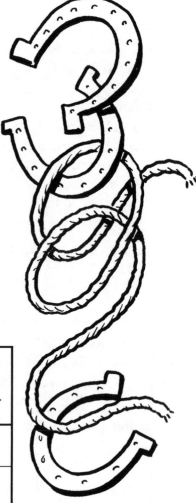

	bridling	leading	roping	saddling	shoeing	March 8	April 12	May 10	June 14	July 12
Bobby										
Denny										
Judy										
Lila										
Trudy										
March 8										
April 12										
May 10										
June 14										
July 12										

Gee, It's Great to Be a Newsboy (or Girl!)

The Woods children (three boys named Fisher, Hunter, and Trapper, and two girls named Flora and Fauna) share a newspaper delivery route. Each child delivers on a different day and has a different mode of transportation. Read the clues to find out which type of transportation each uses during his or her route and the day each child delivers papers.

Clues

1. Hunter delivers the day before Fauna and the day after the boy who delivers by wagon.
2. The child who drives a moped delivers later in the week than the one who pulls a cart.
3. A girl walks her route two days after the one who bikes and one day before Trapper does his delivery.
4. The one who walks the route delivers papers the day after Fauna and the day before Trapper.

	Tuesday	Wednesday	Thursday	Friday	Saturday	bicycle	cart	moped	wagon	walking
Fauna										
Fisher										
Flora										
Hunter										
Trapper										
bicycle										
cart										
moped										
wagon										
walking										

The Guys' Cash Stash

Basil, Edward, Howie, and P.J. have been neighborhood buddies since they were toddlers. Esteban recently moved next door to Howie. To welcome him, the boys decided to purchase five new basketballs, one for each boy. They pooled their spare change and money from small jobs. Read the clues to learn the four boys' first and last names and the amount each was able to contribute.

How much did the boys collect in all? $_____

How much did each new ball cost? $_____

Clues
1. The Mason boy gave ⅓ as much as P.J.
2. Basil's last name is not Carson.
3. Howie could pay more than Basil, but less than the O'Banyon boy.
4. The Carson boy donated three times as much as the Fereday boy could afford.
5. Howie's pocket contained ⅓ as much change as the O'Banyon boy's.

	Carson	Fereday	Mason	O'Banyon	$12.46	$29.54	$37.38	$88.62
Basil								
Edward								
Howie								
P.J.								
$12.46								
$29.54								
$37.38								
$88.62								

Family Reunion

The Larsen family was planning a reunion. On five different days, five relatives purchased different items to bring for the festivities. Calculate the five total amounts each relative spent on his or her items and write them in the matrix (least to greatest is beneficial). Then use the clues to discover which person spent which amount and when he or she bought the items listed in the notes below.

Notes
- One got 5 packages of toilet paper at $1.29 each and 2 board games at $14.95 and $19.95.
- Another purchased 12 packages of cookies at $2.89 each and 4 kites at $1.68 each.
- The third one contributed 6 decks of cards at $.89 each and 7 cases of sodas at $5.35 each.
- One bought 2 bottles of bubbles at $1.89 each and 15 boxes of snack cakes at $2.49 each.
- A fifth person got 9 bags of pretzels at $2.85 each and 8 large bottles of lemonade at $1.99 each.

Clues
1. Bubbles and cakes were bought Friday.
2. Celina purchased items on Monday, but she did not spend $42.79.
3. The one who bought toilet paper and games shopped on Wednesday.
4. Skyler spent $41.40. He shopped the day after Kara.
5. Sophie spent more than $41.25.

Family Reunion, Continued

items ➤										
totals ➤	$	$	$	$	$	Mon.	Tue.	Wed.	Thu.	Fri.
Celina										
Hannah										
Kara										
Skyler										
Sophie										
Mon.										
Tues.										
Wed.										
Thu.										
Fri.										

More Math Logic Mysteries © Prufrock Press Inc.
This page may be photocopied or reproduced with permission for student use.

Math for Moms and Dads

Three moms (Carla, Ellen, and Nyla) and three dads (George, Jude, and Ryne) came to school to tell students how they use math every day in their jobs and why it is important to learn math. Use the clues to discover each parent's career and on which day he or she gave his or her presentation.

Clues

1. Ryne spoke before the seamstress.
2. Ellen spoke before the banker and the computer programmer, but after George.
3. Nyla and Ellen met when one approved a loan for the other to build a sewing shop.
4. The graphic artist spoke after George but before the clerk.
5. Judd spoke about clerking after Mrs. Walton who spoke later than the graphic artist.
6. The clerk spoke 4 weeks ahead of Carla.

	Oct. 3	Oct. 21	Nov. 1	Nov. 14	Nov. 28	Dec. 12	banker	carpet layer	clerk	computer programmer	graphic artist	seamstress
Carla												
Ellen												
George												
Judd												
Nyla												
Ryne												
banker												
carpet layer												
clerk												
computer programmer												
graphic artist												
seamstress												

Am I in the Right Area?

Mr. Frost divided his math class into teams and asked them to guess the area of three rectangles. Team captains (Geoffrey, Kaneisha, and Lin) recorded the team's guesses before they calculated the areas. Change fractions to decimals (numerator ÷ denominator), calculate the areas for the three rectangles (l × w), and write them in the middle row. Find out which team guessed which area for each rectangle. Which team guessed closest to the correct areas for each rectangle?

Clues

1. The team that guessed 139.56 sq. cm. also guessed 70.9 sq. cm. but did not guess 80.2 sq. cm.
2. Lin was not the captain of the team that guessed 139.56 sq. cm. and 87.5 sq. cm. on two answers.
3. The captain who estimated 141.3 sq. cm. also guessed 72.42 sq. cm. but not 72.1 sq. cm.
4. Kaneisha's team guessed 80.2 sq. cm. for the middle rectangle, but was not the team that guessed 139.56 sq. cm. for the largest one.

	Sizes ➤	10 ⅖ cm × 13 ⁹⁄₁₀ cm			9 ⁷⁄₁₀ cm × 8 ⅗ cm			6 ³⁄₁₀ cm × 11 ⅘ cm		
	Calculated Areas ➤	Largest: _____ sq. cm.			Middle: _____ sq. cm.			Smallest: _____ sq. cm.		
	Guesses ➤	133.6 sq. cm	139.56 sq. cm	141.3 sq. cm	72.42 sq. cm	80.2 sq. cm	87.5 sq. cm	68.4 sq. cm	70.9 sq. cm	72.1 sq. cm
	Geoffrey									
	Kaneisha									
	Lin									
smallest	68.4 sq. cm.									
	70.9 sq. cm.									
	72.1 sq. cm.									
middle	72.42 sq. cm.									
	80.2 sq. cm.									
	87.5 sq. cm.									

More Math Logic Mysteries © Prufrock Press Inc.
This page may be photocopied or reproduced with permission for student use.

Teaspoon Trivia

Four neighbor kids were helping with household tasks on Saturday. They took a break to play ball and tell about their chores. They realized they had measured out the same substances for various tasks. Calculate grams (1 tsp = 4.77 grams) for each substance and write them in the "grams" row. Use the clues to determine how much of each substance each child used.

Clues

1. One poured 71.55 grams and one measured 114.48 grams. Nettie was neither of them.
2. The ones who used 171.72 g of detergent and 85.86 g of fertilizer didn't use 14.31 g of sugar.
3. The four were: one who measured 14.31 grams of sugar, one who dumped out 52.47 grams of fertilizer, one who calibrated 143.1 grams of detergent, and Soledad.
4. The one who used 33.39 grams of sugar did not measure 52.47 grams of fertilizer.
5. Graham and Soledad's fertilizer amounts were ½ as much as Farrah and Nettie's detergents.
6. Farrah used more sugar than Soledad, but less than Nettie.

	Sugar				Plant Fertilizer				Laundry Detergent			
tsp ➤	3	5	7	8	11	15	18	23	24	30	36	42
grams ➤												
Farrah												
Graham												
Nettie												
Soledad												
24												
30												
36												
42												
11												
15												
18												
23												

This Fits Me to a T

The Townsend triplets look alike but have very diverse interests. Strangely, they each have a lucky number, volleyball jersey number, and locker number that start with "T." Read the clues to ascertain the lucky number, jersey number and locker number for each girl.

Clues

1. The sister whose lucky number is a multiple of 9 wears a single-digit jersey.
2. Tabitha has an even-numbered jersey and locker number.
3. The sister whose jersey is an "unlucky number" dislikes dodecahedrons.
4. Tonya's lucky number is a multiple of 8, and her locker number is a multiple of 7.
5. The girl whose jersey number is a divisor of another jersey number has a multiple of 9 for her locker number.
6. Terisah's locker is not a multiple of 7.

	lucky number			jersey number			locker number		
	12	24	36	2	10	13	21	28	36
Tabitha									
Terisah									
Tonya									
locker number — 21									
locker number — 28									
locker number — 36									
jersey number — 2									
jersey number — 10									
jersey number — 13									

The Great Chili Cook-Off

Six teams of chili chefs were challenged to create Chillicothe's Choice Chili. Each team's leader divulged that they listen to a specific music genre while cooking, and they told how much of a spicy secret ingredient they use in their recipe. Calculate to determine the missing amounts and write them in the grid (2 Tbsp = 1 ounce and 8 oz. = 1 cup). Read the clues and match each leader with their team's amount of spicy secret ingredient and music preference.

Clues
1. Juanita uses more spice than the R&B fans.
2. The reggae cooks use less spice than Zylo's team.
3. The R & B cooks use more tablespoons of their spice than Faresse's team, but less than the team that uses 30 Tbsp of flavoring.
4. The classical buffs add more ounces of their secret spice than Greta and the rock team's combined, but fewer ounces than Viann's team uses.
5. The Kenny Chesney listeners use ⅕ as much spice as Juanita's team.
6. The reggae listeners use ½ c. less spice than Faresse's team and ⅜ c. more than Greta's team.

							classical	country	hip-hop	R & B	reggae	rock
Cups ➤		¾			2 ¼							
Oz. ➤			10		15							
Tbsp ➤	6			28								
Faresse												
Greta												
Juanita												
Oscar												
Viann												
Zylo												
classical												
country												
hip-hop												
R & B												
reggae												
rock												

Stop and Smell the Roses

Ah, the fragrance of flowers! Men and women, girls and (some) boys like flowers! Three teens (a boy named Clark and two girls named Sonya and Tabby) purchased flowers or plants for loved ones on three holidays last year. Use the clues to match the teens with the amounts they spent on each holiday. Total the three holiday expenditures. Who spent the most money? _____

Clues

1. One teen used her allowance to buy ½ dozen red roses for Valentine's Day. The cost was half as much as Sonya spent on her dad's Father's Day plant.
2. Clark spent three times more for a bouquet of fresh flowers on Mother's Day than Sonya spent on flowers for a different holiday.
3. Tabby spent half as much on pink carnations for one holiday as Clark spent for another holiday.

		Valentine's Day			Mother's Day			Father's Day		
		$16.38	$17.46	$65.96	$18.49	$49.14	$65.52	$34.92	$36.98	$52.38
	Clark									
	Sonya									
	Tabby									
Father's Day	$34.92									
	$36.98									
	$52.38									
Mother's Day	$18.49									
	$49.14									
	$65.52									

What's Your E.T.A.?

Four friends flew from Seattle, WA, on the same day to visit grandparents who live in different cities and states. Use the clues to discover each child's flight departure time and estimated time of arrival (E.T.A.). After you solve the puzzle, calculate to find the difference between each child's departure and arrival. Who had the shortest and longest trips? Time zones and layovers affected the lengths of some trips.

Shortest: _____   Longest: _____

Clues

1. The one who arrived at 2:47 p.m. departed earlier than Catava, but later than Jacy.
2. The one who departed at 5:24 a.m. did not arrive at 1:59 p.m.
3. Catava's E.T.A. was about 13 hrs later than Manning's departure time.
4. Manning arrived later than the one who departed at 9:18 a.m., but earlier than the one who departed at 6:51 a.m.
5. The one who arrived at 1:59 p.m. did not depart at 12:03 a.m.

	Departure Time				Arrival Time			
	12:03 a.m.	5:24 a.m.	6:51 a.m.	9:18 a.m.	8:04 a.m.	1:59 p.m.	2:47 p.m.	6:25 p.m.
Catava								
Jacy								
Manning								
Sutton								
8:04 a.m.								
1:59 p.m.								
2:47 p.m.								
6:25 p.m.								

Sunny Side Up

Service Club members take turns volunteering at the pool to help watch swimmers. Fujita and six others guarded during a summer heat wave. To make it seem cooler outside, they thought about the temperature in Celsius degrees, a different temperature scale. Convert Celsius to Fahrenheit using the formula below. Round to nearest whole numbers and write Fahrenheit degree in the chart. *Hint:* Check your work using the Fahrenheit to Celsius formula. Then, read the clues and determine which volunteer guarded on which day.

Notes

When you know Celsius temperature: $F = (\frac{9}{5} \times C^\circ) + 32$
For example: 100° C is $(\frac{9}{5} \times 100) + 32$, and $\frac{9}{5}$ is 1.8, so $\frac{9}{5}$ (1.8) $\times$ 100 = 180 + 32, or 212° F.

When you know Fahrenheit temperature: $C = \frac{5}{9} \times (F^\circ - 32)$
For example: 100° F is $\frac{5}{9} \times (100 - 32)$ and $\frac{5}{9}$ is .555, so $\frac{5}{9}$ (.555) $\times$ 68 = 38° C.

Clues

1. Fujita's duty was during a hotter day than Courtney's, but not as hot as Thatcher's.
2. Bolton watched on a day when the Fahrenheit temperature was exactly six times his age.
3. Kipp guarded on a day when the Fahrenheit temperature was seven times his age.
4. LaRae's day was hotter than Jayvyn's, but cooler than Bolton's and Kipp's days.
5. Jayvyn watched on a day when the Fahrenheit temperature was five times his age.
6. LaRae served on a day when the Fahrenheit temperature was four times her age.

Sunny Side Up, Continued

Celsius ➤	32.22°	32.77°	33.33°	34.44°	35.55°	36.66°	37.77°
Fahrenheit ➤							
Bolton							
Courtney							
Fujita							
Jayvyn							
Kipp							
LaRae							
Thatcher							

Vital Statistics

The school nurse has completed her check of all students' height and weight. The Singh family (three girls named Avaia, Chaitra, and Elina, and three boys named Devitri, Kavi, and Rishab) received the report that all of the children were in the average range. Use the clues to match each child with his or her height and weight.

Clues

1. Rishab weighs 109 lbs.
2. Elina is taller than the girl who weighs 116 lbs.
3. Neither Devitri nor the boy who weighs 145 lbs is 4' 6" or 4' 11".
4. Rishab is shorter than Chaitra who is not as tall as either the girl who weighs 134 lbs or Elina.
5. The boy who weighs 123 lbs is 2" taller than the girl who weighs 118 lbs.
6. Kavi is not as tall as Avaia.

	Height						Weight					
	4' 6"	4' 8"	4' 11"	5' 1"	5' 5"	5' 9"	109 lbs	116 lbs	118 lbs	123 lbs	134 lbs	145 lbs
Avaia												
Chaitra												
Devitri												
Elina												
Kavi												
Rishab												
109 lbs												
116 lbs												
118 lbs												
123 lbs												
134 lbs												
145 lbs												

More Math Logic Mysteries © Prufrock Press Inc.

Fraction Action

Seven of Mr. Ike's math students created a game called "Fraction Action." Each wrote a fraction (⁴⁄₁₅, ⁵⁄₁₈, ⁷⁄₂₆, ⁸⁄₂₉, ⁹⁄₃₃, ¹¹⁄₄₀, and ¹³⁄₄₇) on a card and then asked their classmates to place the seven cards in order from smallest to largest. One quick thinker calculated decimal equivalents (divide numerator by denominator) and could rapidly sequence the cards. Calculate equivalents of the seven fractions to the nearest thousandths. Write the fractions and decimals in order from smallest to largest on the grid, according to the decimal numbers, rounding to the nearest thousandths place. Then, use clues to identify which student wrote each fraction card.

Clues

1. Fritz wrote a fraction whose decimal equivalent was .002 < Isabel's.
2. Kathleen's fraction was > Isabel's and < Craig's.
3. Marjorie did not write ⁷⁄₂₆ or the fraction whose decimal equivalent was .277.
4. Neither Isabel nor Marjorie wrote ⁴⁄₁₅ or the fraction whose decimal equivalent was .275.
5. Craig's fraction was < Luther's but > Marjorie's.
6. Grace wrote a fraction whose decimal equivalent was .002 > Kathleen's.
7. The one who wrote ⁸⁄₂₉, Grace's fraction, and the one whose decimal equivalent was .278 are in consecutive order.

fractions ➤							
decimals ➤							
Craig							
Fritz							
Grace							
Isabel							
Kathleen							
Luther							
Marjorie							

The Coin Collectors

Four students in Ms. Frank's math class (two girls named Eileen and Nadia, and two boys named Santos and Trevor) are beginning numismatists. They have each collected different numbers of dimes and quarters. Calculate the values for the dimes and quarters, and write the totals in the boxes beside "values." Use the clues to determine each student's first and last name, and the number of coins in his or her collection. Find the total values of the four collections.

Clues

1. Nobody's first and last name start with the same letter.
2. The number of dimes or quarters a child has does not start with the same letter as his or her first or last name (for example, 11 dimes isn't Eileen or Edo). The number of dimes and quarters don't start with the same letter (for example, 91 dimes does not go with 92 quarters).
3. Nadia has 17 fewer dimes than the one who had 34 quarters.
4. Nadia has half as many quarters as the boy who had 28 dimes.
5. The Nim child has 17 fewer dimes in his collection than the Edo child.

		last name				number of dimes				number of quarters			
				values ➤		$	$	$	$	$	$	$	$
		Edo	Nim	Spar	Topp	11	28	74	91	34	46	68	92
	Eileen												
	Nadia												
	Santos												
	Trevor												
number of quarters	34												
	46												
	68												
	92												
number of dimes	11												
	28												
	74												
	91												

Shop 'Til You Stop

Five kids rode their bikes to Dollar Department Den to make a small purchase. Each bought a different item and shopped at a different time of day. Use the clues to ferret out who bought what item and the time each one shopped for it.

Clues

1. One purchased baseball cards at 5:30.
2. Chuck shopped at 9:00, but he didn't buy soda.
3. Someone bought a candy bar at 1:15 p.m.
4. Paulette did not buy baseball cards.
5. Lymon bought crayons. He began shopping 2 ¾ hours later than Hixon.

	baseball cards	candy bar	crayons	dog food	soda	9:00 a.m.	10:30 a.m.	1:15 p.m.	4:00 p.m.	5:30 p.m.
Chuck										
Donnita										
Hixon										
Lymon										
Paulette										
9:00 a.m.										
10:30 a.m.										
1:15 p.m.										
4:00 p.m.										
5:30 p.m.										

Summer Sitters

Three friends each enjoy caring for young children. During one week of summer vacation, each had three different sitting jobs on the same days, but for different lengths of time. Calculate the length of each job and write it in the "total time" row. Use the clues to determine who sat for how long on each day. Each girl earned $3.50 per hour for her work. Who made the most money that week?

Clues

1. Kamea sat from 2:15–8:45 p.m. on Thursday.
2. Someone sat from 1:00–6:15 p.m. Monday and for less than 6 hours on Saturday.
3. Tatum sat for 6h 15m on Monday.
4. One girl sat starting at 1:45 p.m. on Monday and 3:45 p.m. on Thursday.
5. The one who sat 3:30–9:15 p.m. on Saturday sat less than 5 hours Thursday.
6. Tatum made more money than Kamea.

Summer Sitters, Continued

	Monday			Thursday			Saturday		
Sitting job ➤	1:00–6:15 p.m.	4:30–10:15 p.m.	1:45–8:00 p.m.	5:00–9:30 p.m.	3:45–9:30 p.m.	2:15–8:45 p.m.	3:30–9:15 p.m.	1:15–7:30 p.m.	2:45–9:45 p.m.
Total Time ➤	hrs min	hrs min	hrs min	hrs min	hrs min	hrs min	hrs min	hrs min	hrs min
Kamea									
Lari									
Tatum									
Saturday 3:30–9:15									
Saturday 1:15–7:30									
Saturday 2:45–9:45									
Thursday 5:00–9:30									
Thursday 3:45–9:30									
Thursday 2:15–8:45									

Arduous Arithmetic

Mr. Marsh commences each Monday morning with menacing math! Whoever correctly solves both problems first earns the moniker "Math Marvel" for the week. Four girls tackled last week's problems, which required them to convert miles to kilometers and pounds to kilograms. Convert fractions to decimals (numerator ÷ denominator). Divide miles by ⅝ (.625) as 1 kilometer (km) = ⅝ mi and pounds by 2.2046 as 1 kilogram (kg) = 2.2046 pounds. Fill in the "My answers" row. If you calculated correctly, you will be able to use the clues to find out which two problems each girl solved and identify who was named last week's "Math Marvel."

Clues

1. Blaire did not calculate 5 miles or figure 22.046 pounds.
2. The one who converted 6 ⅞ miles (not Sabah) did not guess 10 kg (not Ashley).
3. Four students were: the one who converted 8 ⅛ mi., the girl who calculated 22.046 pounds, one who found 8 km as an answer, and Maya.
4. The girl who did the 5-mile problem liked converting 30.8644 pounds into kilograms.
5. Maya converted less weight than Blaire.

Problems ➤		3 ¾ miles	5 miles	6 ⅞ miles	8 ⅛ miles	6.6138 pounds	17.6368 pounds	22.046 pounds	30.8644 pounds
My answers ➤		km	km	km	km	kg	kg	kg	kg
Students' answers ➤		6 km	8 km	10.75 km	12 km	3.75 kg	8 kg	10 kg	13 kg
	Ashley								
	Blaire								
	Maya								
	Sabah								
6.6138 pounds	3.75 kg								
17.6368 pounds	8 kg								
22.046 pounds	10 kg								
30.8644 pounds	13 kg								

Winter in Wyoming

Eight classmates from Cody, WY, all have birthdays in January. For math class, they tracked the unusually cold temperatures on their birthdays. Read the clues and use the number line to help you deduce the temperature on each one's birthday. (Moving left is colder and right is warmer.)

Clues

1. It was four degrees colder on L'Wella's birthday than Ruby's.
2. The temperature on Aidan's birthday was four degrees colder than Dori's.
3. The temperature on Trista's birthday was warmer than Bentley's and Hope's, but cooler than Dori's and Forbes' birthdays.
4. The temperature on Ruby's birthday was four degrees colder than Forbes'.
5. It was cooler on Dori's birthday than it was on Forbes' and L'Wella's, but it was warmer on Dori's birthday than it was on Aidan's whose day was warmer than Hope's.
6. The temperature on Bentley's birthday was four degrees colder than Aidan's.

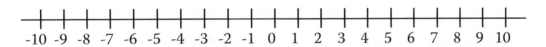

	-9°	-7°	-5°	-2°	-1°	2°	6°	10°
Aidan								
Bentley								
Dori								
Forbes								
Hope								
L'Wella								
Ruby								
Trista								

Triathlon Times

The Taylor family is very physically fit. They bike together nearly every day. Two children go out for cross-country at school, and two are on swim team during the summer. The town of Tyler sponsored a nonstandard team triathlon, but the Taylors entered as individuals. Use the clues to discover the times each child clocked for each event. You will find it helpful to convert minute and second times into seconds before multiplying or dividing (for example, 4m 32s = 272 seconds.

Clues

1. The one who ran for 18m 27s is not the one who swam for 6m 4s or the one who biked for 29m 29s.
2. Elery swam ¼ as long as he biked.
3. Perry swam ⅓ as long as Alana ran.
4. The one who biked for 26m 15s ran for 18m 12s, but did not swim the fastest.
5. Kalista ran for exactly 2 minutes more than three times her swim time.

		biking				running				swimming			
		21m 09s	23m 44s	26m 15s	29m 29s	17m 51s	18m 12s	18m 27s	20m 13s	5m 17s	5m 56s	5m 59s	6m 04s
	Alana												
	Elery												
	Kalista												
	Perry												
swimming	5m 17s												
	5m 56s												
	5m 59s												
	6m 04s												
running	17m 51s												
	18m 12s												
	18m 27s												
	20m 13s												

Name: .... Date: ....

Exponent² Components³

Each day last week Miss Cubely, the math teacher, gave one student a different exponential problem to solve. Three girls named Cheri, Elena, and Janna, and two boys named Mannix and Rusty each calculated one problem. Write the cubes (2^3 is $2 \times 2 \times 2 = 8$, for example) in the grid and use the clues to find out who solved which problem on which day.

Clues

1. Either the student who calculated 4^3 or Rusty did Tuesday's problem.
2. Elena's answer was 216, but she didn't solve her problem on Wednesday.
3. The student whose answer was 343 did a problem the day after Cheri.
4. A girl did not get 64 for an answer.
5. Rusty did a problem a day after Mannix.
6. The one who did 5^3 did not solve a problem the day before Janna.
7. Either the one who did 7^3 or Mannix did Friday's problem.

	3^3	4^3	5^3	6^3	7^3	Mon.	Tue.	Wed.	Thu.	Fri.
Cheri										
Elena										
Janna										
Mannix										
Rusty										
Mon.					
Tue.					
Wed.					
Thu.					
Fri.					

What Goes Around Comes Around

Each Friday afternoon, Miss Brendan asks students to practice rounding numbers. Last week's problems required students to round numbers to the nearest hundreds. Round the original numbers and write your answers in the empty boxes. Compare them with the students' answers, and then use the clues to discover which problem each student solved. Which students correctly rounded, and what mistakes were made by other students? How did you do?

Clues

1. Elizabeth's number was larger than Steve's but smaller than Nelson's.
2. Rush and Elizabeth rounded 5-digit numbers while Faye and Yvette were assigned 4-digit or 6-digit numbers.
3. Kent's number was smaller than Clarice's but larger than Faye's, and Nelson's was larger than Yvette's whose number was larger than Rush's.
4. Elizabeth's number was smaller than Kent's 5-digit number, and Rush's number was larger than Clarice's 5-digit number.
5. One number was exactly divisible by Faye's.

Original number ➤	2,653	4,892	10,393	13,651	68,978	96,102	587,932	716,294
Your answers ➤								
Students' answers ➤	2,655	4,800	10,400	13,700	68,000	100,000	587,900	716,290
Clarice								
Elizabeth								
Faye								
Kent								
Nelson								
Rush								
Steve								
Yvette								

Let's Hit the Slopes

Five friends went skiing for a day at Heavenly Hills Ski Resort. Each bought used ski boots and jackets for the outing. Use the clues to determine which skier bought which boots and jacket. Who spent the least? _____
Who spent the most? _____

Clues

1. Kipley's boots cost ½ as much as either Tamiko's boots or Tamiko's jacket.
2. Of the skiers wearing $168 and $148 jackets, neither paid half those amounts for his or her boots.
3. Someone spent three times as much for his or her jacket as he or she did on boots.
4. Prita's boots cost $51 less than Darlis' jacket, and Darlis' boots cost $51 less than Tamiko's jacket.
5. Prita's jacket cost the same as Kipley's boots and jacket combined.
6. Tamiko's jacket cost the same as her boots and Prita's boots combined.

	Ski Boots					Ski Jackets				
	$56	$74	$84	$112	$135	$125	$148	$168	$186	$224
Darlis										
Kipley										
Max										
Prita										
Tamiko										
$125					
$148					
$168					
$186					
$224					

My Space

Math students measured the area of their bedrooms and calculated their annual allowances. Four students promptly completed their assignments. Calculate bedroom area (sq ft = length × width) and allowances (weekly rate × 52 weeks), and write the amounts in the chart. Use appropriate labels. Read the clues to match each student with his or her age, bedroom area, and allowance.

Clues

1. The 12-year-old's bedroom is not 132 sq. ft. or 156 sq. ft.
2. Neither Nate nor the 10-year-old has an 11 ft. × 12 ft. bedroom.
3. The one who has a 11 ft. × 14 ft. bedroom does not earn $143 per year or $3.50 per week (which is not the 11-year-old's rate).
4. Neither Nate's nor Lydia's bedroom is 13 ft. × 15 ft.
5. The 12-year-old doesn't have a 13 ft. × 15 ft. bedroom or get $234 per year for allowance.
6. The four friends are: one whose bedroom is 12 ft. × 13 ft., one who gets $2.75 per week, the 11-year-old, and Dwight.

My Space, Continued

	Age (years)				Bedroom Size (feet)				Weekly Allowance			
	10	11	12	13	11 × 12	11 × 14	12 × 13	13 × 15	$2.75	$3.50	$4.50	$5.25
Sq. ft. ➤									$	$	$	$
Dwight												
Lydia												
Nate												
Twyla												
$2.75												
$3.50												
$4.50												
$5.25												
11 × 12												
11 × 14												
12 × 13												
13 × 15												

Land of 10,000 Lakes

Five families from Minneapolis, MN, traveled over Labor Day weekend to visit relatives and friends in three other Minnesota cities. Use the clues to learn each family's first, second, and third stops during their trips. You also may want to check a mileage chart and/or consult a map.

Clues

1. One family drove 63 miles from Rochester to Albert Lea, but it wasn't the Gilmans.
2. One family drove 137 miles from Moorhead to Brainerd, but it wasn't the Clausens.
3. The Medfords drove 99 miles to Red Wing, but it wasn't from Hibbing or Willmar.
4. The Clausens visited Hutchinson and the Gilmans drove to Duluth, but neither family drove to Brainerd.
5. The Hennepins and Medfords were not the ones who visited three cities that start with the letter M.
6. The family who drove 58 miles to Willmar also drove 109 miles to Fergus Falls, but it wasn't Hennepins or Gilmans.

Land of 10,000 Lakes, Continued

		First Stop					Second Stop					Third Stop				
		Duluth	Hutchinson	Mankato	Rochester	St. Cloud	Albert Lea	Hibbing	Marshall	Moorhead	Willmar	Brainerd	Fergus Falls	International Falls	Montevideo	Red Wing
	Clausen															
	Faribault															
	Gilman															
	Hennepin															
	Medford															
Third Stop	Brainerd															
	Fergus Falls															
	Int'l. Falls															
	Montevideo															
	Red Wing															
Second Stop	Albert Lea															
	Hibbing															
	Marshall															
	Moorhead															
	Willmar															

Speed Doesn't Pay, You Do!

Two women (Larissa and Melissa) and two men learned that exceeding a 55 mph speed limit is costly. Each was fined $5, $6, $7, or $8 for each mile per hour they were speeding over the limit. Use those costs to calculate and mark the total fine/mph over limit section first. Find the time each driver was ticketed, how many mph over the limit he or she was driving, and his or her total fine.

Clues

1. Justin was ticketed 7 hrs. 8 min. earlier than Melissa.
2. The one ticketed on the way to open her store at the mall was driving faster than Travis, who did not pay $80. Travis' cost was not $7 for each mph over.
3. Justin's cost was higher for each mph over the limit than Larissa's, but she paid a higher total fine.
4. The one who received a ticket on the way home from teaching sixth grade did not pay a $126 fine.
5. The driver ticketed 7 hrs. 8 min. before the one who paid $96 was not driving 16 mph over the limit.

	Time of day ticketed				Miles per hour over limit				Total fine			
	2:13 a.m.	9:21 a.m.	4:29 p.m.	11:37 p.m.	12 mph	15 mph	16 mph	18 mph	$80	$90	$96	$126
Justin												
Larissa												
Melissa												
Travis												
$80												
$90												
$96												
$126												
12 mph												
15 mph												
16 mph												
18 mph												

◄ Complete this section first. Use $5, $6, $7, and $8 costs to calculate mph and total fines. Example: $70 ÷ $5 = 14 mph over. Check solutions to be certain your calculations are correct before solving.

Let's Hit the Road, Girls

Four friends and their sisters were treated to a special weekend with their moms. Each family drove to a different destination. They spent various amounts on gas, the motel, and shopping. Use the clues to match each girl with the amounts her family spent during their excursion.

Clues

1. Heidi's mom spent $8.66 less on gas than Kat's, but Kat's mom spent less on motel and shopping than Heidi's.
2. Meredith's mom spent $4.87 more on motel than Kat's and $8.66 more on gas than Kat's.
3. One family spent exactly seven times more on shopping than the motel.
4. One group spent $5.47 less on gas than motel.
5. Maggie's mom spent ⅛ as much on gas as Heidi's family spent shopping.
6. One family spent a difference of $318.91 between shopping and the motel.

	Gasoline				Motel				Shopping			
	$55.29	$63.95	$72.61	$81.27	$59.68	$64.55	$69.42	$74.29	$368.64	$393.20	$417.76	$442.32
Heidi												
Kat												
Maggie												
Meredith												
Shopping $368.64												
Shopping $393.20												
Shopping $417.76												
Shopping $442.32												
Motel $59.68												
Motel $64.55												
Motel $69.42												
Motel $74.29												

Sweet Treat

Care Club members (two boys named Carnine and Ramsey and three girls named Emma, Jenntrie, and Naomi) recently held a benefit for a sick friend. Each made different candies and sold different weights and amounts of them. Complete the chart above the matrix as you read clues (weight × price per pound = total price). Convert fractions to decimals such as ¼ = .25. Identify who sold how much of each candy for which price. *Note:* A clue that says 25% more means one whole amount plus 25%. For example, 1 + .25 = 1.25, so 25% more than $3.00 = 3 × 1.25 or $3.75. A clue that says 100% more means 1 plus 100% (1 + 1 = 2 times the amount). A clue that says 25% as much means one whole amount minus 25% (or 1 − .25 = .75 times the amount).

Clues

1. The cashew clusters sold for $5 per pound.
2. Ramsey made 50% as much money on his chocolate cherries as Emma did on her treat.
3. The caramels sold for 75% less per pound than the 2½ lbs of fudge at $3 per pound.
4. A girl sold 100% more pounds of brittle than the one who made chocolate cherries.
5. Ramsey sold 50% fewer pounds of candy than the boy who made cashew clusters.
6. Jenntrie earned 20% as much as Carnine.

More Math Logic Mysteries © Prufrock Press Inc.
This page may be photocopied or reproduced with permission for student use.

Sweet Treat, Continued

	caramels	cashew cluster	chocolate cherries	vanilla fudge	peanut brittle
Cook					
Weight	lbs	lbs	lbs	lbs	lbs
Price per lb.	$ per lb	$ per lb	$ per lb	$ per lb	$ per lb
Total price	$	$	$	$	$

	weight					total price				
	1 ½ lbs	2 ½ lbs	3 lbs	3 lbs	4 lbs	$3.00	$5.25	$7.50	$10.50	$15.00
Carnine										
Emma										
Jenntrie										
Naomi										
Ramsey										
$3.00										
$5.25										
$7.50										
$10.50										
$15.00										

Flower Power

Twelve Garden Society members were expecting babies. Each pledged a donation to the new Botanical Center that would be the numerical representation of her wedding anniversary times the child's day of birth (for example: 5-13 (May 13) × ~~June~~ 8 is 513 × 8 = $4,104; 2-6 (Feb. 6) × ~~April~~ 30 is 26 × 30 = $780; and 11-3 (Nov. 3) × ~~March~~ 25 is 113 × 25 = $2,825). Calculate the amounts, and complete the chart. Amazingly, all 12 women had girls, and each daughter was given a floral name. Use the clues to determine each girl's birth date, her mom's donation, and her parents' anniversary. What was the total of all 12 donations? $_____

Clues

1. Dahlia was born in January, April, or June. Jasmine and Violet were born in March or April. All three girls' moms donated more than $5,000.
2. Amaryllis, Laurel, Rosa, or Violet's parents were wed May 24.
3. Rosa, Lily, Iris, and Amaryllis' moms donated less than $4,000.
4. Zinnia, Heather, or Camellia was born on April 4.
5. Heather, Jasmine, Lily, and Zinnia's moms gave $3,000–$6,000.
6. Dahlia's mother contributed $8 less than twice Heather's mom's donation.
7. Heather's mom gave $108 more than double Rosa's mother.
8. Camellia was born 2 weeks after her parents' anniversary.
9. Ginger was born 9 days before her parents' anniversary.

Flower Power, Continued

	Mar. 2	Apr. 13	June 21	June 19	May 27	Jan. 15	Feb. 28	Apr. 4	Mar. 17	May 6	Apr. 30	Jan. 8
amount ➤ $												
anniversary date ➤	5-24	9-7	6-7	8-4	6-5	2-20	12-6	12-25	3-23	10-21	2-14	8-24
day of birth ➤												
Amaryllis												
Camellia												
Dahlia												
Ginger												
Heather												
Iris												
Jasmine												
Laurel												
Lily												
Rosa												
Violet												
Zinnia												

Out to Lunch: Part I

Mr. Brega took his daughters (Carrie and Merrie) and sons (Barry and Gary) to lunch. He had $26.40 to divide evenly. How much was each person allotted? $_____ Dad spent his entire share. The grid shows what fraction of his or her allotment each child spent. Divide numerators by denominators to get decimals (for example, ⅝ = .625). Multiply allotments × decimals to calculate the amounts spent. Write totals beside "amounts spent" and in the lower grid. Subtract amounts spent from the allotment to find out how much change each child received, and write that in the top row of boxes. Use the clues to discover which meal each child ordered and how much it cost.

Clues

1. One ate mozzarella cheese sticks.
2. Barry's burger and fries order did not leave him with $0.88 change.
3. Neither Carrie nor the one who ate salad and milk spent $4.40.
4. One had $1.32 in change after she bought fruit for her lunch.
5. The boy who had salad did not have $1.76 left.
6. Carrie is a vegetarian.

		burger & fries	chicken & fruit	mozz. & fruit	salad & milk	change ➤ $ ⅝	$ ⅔	$ ¾	$ ⅚
						amounts spent ➤ $	$	$	$
	Barry								
	Carrie								
	Gary								
	Merrie								
⅝	$								
⅔	$								
¾	$								
⅚	$								

You will need information from this puzzle to solve "Out to Lunch: Part II" on the following page.

Out to Lunch: Part II

After lunch, the Brega kids planned to go to the mall with friends (two boys named Jamason and Momed, and two girls named Adrienne and Necia). Each wanted to make a small purchase with the change from their meals, but they all misplaced their money. Fortunately, each friend found the change, but in different locations. Analyze the clues to learn which friend found the money in which location and how much could be spent on which item. It may be helpful to jot notes beside some information. You will need to refer to "Out to Lunch: Part I" to complete this puzzle.

Clues

1. The one who ate salad lost his change in the garage. He did not plan to buy a deck of cards or pencils with his change.
2. Merrie and her friend did not find her change on the bedroom dresser or plan to spend it on a milkshake.
3. Adrienne went with her friend to buy a new deck of cards.
4. The boys found change in the car and planned to buy pencils for school with the money.
5. Momed's friend had $\frac{1}{6}$ of the money left, just enough to buy clips for her hair.

	location of money				change from lunch allotment			
	bed-room	car	coat pocket	garage floor	$\frac{1}{6}$	$\frac{1}{4}$	$\frac{1}{3}$	$\frac{3}{8}$
					$	$	$	$
Adrienne								
Jamason								
Momed								
Necia								
$\frac{1}{6}$ $								
$\frac{1}{4}$ $								
$\frac{1}{3}$ $								
$\frac{3}{8}$ $								

You Can Bank on This

Four sisters made various deposits at their banks. Each receives a different rate of interest at the end of the month. Read the clues to learn who uses which bank and how much interest she will receive on her deposit. Calculate totals (deposit × rate of interest). Subtract the deposits from the totals to discover how much interest each sister earned. Write their interest incomes below.

Chandra $_____   Indira $_____
Malati $_____   Yamini $_____

Clues

1. $175 was deposited at State Bank or Bank of U.S.
2. Bank of U.S. pays .75% less interest than Yamini's bank.
3. The West Trust customer deposited $75 more than the one gets 6.5% interest.
4. The girl who went to State Bank added less money to her account than Malati.
5. Chandra deposited at least $75 more than the sister who will get 5.75% interest.

	Name of Bank				Rate of Interest				Amount of Deposit			
	Bank of U.S.	Lincoln Savings	State Bank	West Trust	5%	5.75%	6.5%	7%	$100	$125	$175	$250
Chandra												
Indira												
Malati												
Yamini												
Deposit $100												
Deposit $125												
Deposit $175												
Deposit $250												
Interest 5%												
Interest 5.75%												
Interest 6.5%												
Interest 7%												

More Math Logic Mysteries © Prufrock Press Inc.
This page may be photocopied or reproduced with permission for student use.

Vacation Vertigo

Five families met in a large hotel while on vacation. Each family stayed on a different floor and had different room numbers. Can you use the clues to verify which family stayed where?

Clues

1. The White family was on a lower floor than the family in room 2164, which was not the Browns.
2. The Grays stayed on a higher floor than the family whose room number was exactly 259 times their floor, which was not the Golds.
3. The Grays stayed on a lower floor than the ones whose room number was higher than the Greens.
4. One family's room number was exactly 165 times their floor number, but it wasn't the Gold family or the Brown family.
5. One family stayed in a room number that was 255 times their floor number.

	3rd floor	8th floor	9th floor	15th floor	23rd floor	Room 2072	Room 2164	Room 2295	Room 2381	Room 2475
Gold										
Brown										
Gray										
Green										
White										
Room 2072										
Room 2164										
Room 2295										
Room 2381										
Room 2475										

Bike-a-Thon

Friends entered a Bike-a-Thon to raise money for leukemia research. Three girls (Camryn, Fylecia, and Lexie) got pledges from family for each mile they rode, and three boys (Benjie, John, and Wallace) secured pledges from friends. Use information from the clues to find the distance each child biked, his or her pledge per mile, and his or her total donation. Add all six bikers' totals together to discover the amount these friends donated. How much was it?
$_____

Pledge and Distance Chart

This chart shows all possible donations. Multiply each pledge by each distance, and finish the chart by writing in your calculations. Total donations ranged from $12.83 to $28.00, so mark out any totals that are less than $12.83 or more than $28.00. Some have been marked for you. Circle totals that are correct amounts such as $12.83 in the gray box. You also know $28.00 is correct. Use your calculations and information from clues to solve the matrix puzzle. You can mark 2.7 mi. as corresponding with $4.75 pledge on your matrix, based on the information below.

D × P = Total		distance ridden					
		2.7 mi	3.2 mi	3.9 mi	4.4 mi	4.9 mi	5.6 mi
pledges per mile	$3.50		$11.20				
	$4.25						
	$4.75	$12.83					
	$5.00						
	$5.30						
	$5.67						$31.75

Bike-a-Thon, Continued

Clues

(Be aware if it says a pledge or a total. Consult your chart for total amounts.)

1. Benjie's pledge and his total donation were both less than John's.
2. Camryn rode ½ mile less than the girl who donated $16.96.
3. Fylecia's donation was more than John's.
4. The child who rode 3.2 miles had a higher pledge than Fylecia, but lower than John. She earned less than Fylecia and John.
5. Wallace's total was $3.87 higher than Lexie's, but his pledge was lower than hers.
6. Wallace rode farther than Benjie who rode farther than John but none of them rode as far as Fylecia.

	distance ridden						pledges per mile					
	2.7 mi	3.2 mi	3.9 mi	4.4 mi	4.9 mi	5.6 mi	$3.50	$4.25	$4.75	$5.00	$5.30	$5.67
Benjie												
Camryn												
Fylecia												
John												
Lexie												
Wallace												
$3.50												
$4.25												
$4.75												
$5.00												
$5.30												
$5.67												

(left label: pledges per mile)

Put It in the Bank

One day six buddies biked to the bank to deposit birthday, allowance, and job money. Bryant said, "Did I ever tell you guys that my last name is the same as the college where my father graduated, and my first name is the university where my mother graduated?" "Mine is too," each boy chimed in. They enjoyed telling the others about this rare happenstance. From the clues, can you discover each boy's first and last collegiate names, plus how much money each deposited?

Clues

1. Cameron deposited half as much as Bryant.
2. Judson took more than Cameron, but less than Reed.
3. Reed deposited less than Mr. Clarke and Mr. Baker.
4. Bryant had more than Reed, who had more than Mr. Morris.
5. Judson took ½ as much as Baker, but more than Mr. DeVry.
6. Mr. DeVry deposited less than half as much as Malloy who did not deposit the most.
7. Mr. Baker put in twice as much as Mr. Morris.
8. Mr. Ferris took ½ as much as Lee who is not Hastings.

	Baker	Clarke	DeVry	Ferris	Hastings	Morris	$82.11	$98.74	$102.68	$164.22	$197.48	$205.36
	Last Name						**Money Deposited**					
Bryant												
Cameron												
Judson												
Lee												
Malloy												
Reed												
$82.11						
$98.74						
$102.68						
$164.22						
$197.48						
$205.36						

More Math Logic Mysteries © Prufrock Press Inc.
This page may be photocopied or reproduced with permission for student use.

Lightning Leap

An issue of *Car and Driver Magazine* compared several sports cars. The cars were unmodified, but had performance-enhancing options such as larger brakes and stiffer suspensions. Match each car with its Brake Horsepower (BHP) and weight that were reported in the magazine.

Clues

1. The Audi has more BHP than the car weighing 3,303 lbs.
2. The Corvette has 100 more BHP than the BMW but the "Vette" weighs 76 lbs. less.
3. The Shelby has at least 20 more BHP than the Porsche.
4. The Porsche weighs more than the car with 400 BHP.
5. The model with 300 BHP weighs 76 pounds more than the Corvette.
6. The sportster with 500 HP outweighs the Porsche by more than 600 pounds.

	300 BHP	400 BHP	415 BHP	420 BHP	500 BHP	3,290 lbs	3,303 lbs	3,366 lbs	3,592 lbs	3,908 lbs
Audi										
BMW										
Corvette										
Ford Shelby										
Porsche										
3,290 lbs										
3,303 lbs										
3,366 lbs										
3,592 lbs										
3,908 lbs										

I Beg Your PARdon

The Quandt siblings attended opening day at the new golf course, where celebrity golfer Cheetah Forest was playing. Each sibling (including two girls, Fran and Rochelle) shot three bogies (1 over par) along with birdies (1 under), pars, double bogies (2 over), and/or triple bogies (3 over). The scorecard shows results from some holes. Read the clues to deduce the missing data, enter it on the scorecard, and add the scores from each hole to find the totals. Who won this game (lowest score)?

Clues

1. Fran and Lawson bogied three consecutive holes.
2. Nobody bogied on Holes 2 or 6, but Ira had par on one of them. He wasn't the one who scored 49.
3. Lawson made his only double bogie on Hole 1 and Fran made her only birdie on Hole 1.
4. Ira and Rochelle birdied on Hole 1 and Hole 6.
5. Wheeler, Ira, and Fran made a double bogie on Hole 5, and Wheeler and Fran each had one other double bogie on an odd-numbered hole.
6. Lawson made two triple bogies in a row.
7. Ira made par on two even-numbered holes and Wheeler had two triple bogies on evens.
8. Five golfers were: three who bogied on Holes 3, 4, and 9; 3, 4, and 8; and 1, 7, and 8; the one who triple bogied on Hole 4; and Lawson.
9. One sister shot double bogies on Holes 2 and 9.

SCORECARD

Par ➤	5	3	4	4	3	5	3	4	4	
Hole ➤	1	2	3	4	5	6	7	8	9	Scores
Fran		3			5					
Ira							6		5	
Lawson						5			4	
Rochelle					3		3			
Wheeler			4	4						

More Math Logic Mysteries © Prufrock Press Inc.
This page may be photocopied or reproduced with permission for student use.

Jean "Green"

Even though they live in different cities, four male cousins are very close and communicate quite frequently. On different days last week each cousin e-mailed the others to say that he had gone shopping for new jeans. The jeans had different tag prices and percents of tax. Read the clues to discover who shopped on what day, the tag price and sales tax each one was charged.

Clues

1. Tuesday's shopper was not Lowe nor the boy who paid 6.5% tax for his jeans tagged $36.99.
2. Blake shopped on Tuesday or Wednesday.
3. Gage purchased his jeans on Tuesday or Thursday.
4. The $36.99 jeans were not bought on Thursday, but were bought some time after Roy bought his and after the one who paid 5.5% tax.
5. Of the boys who shopped Monday and Thursday, one paid 6% tax and one purchased $37.69 jeans.
6. The $36.25 jeans had 7% tax added to their cost.

		Shopping Day				Percent Sales Tax				Tag Price			
		Monday	Tuesday	Wednesday	Thursday	5.5%	6%	6.5%	7%	$34.75	$36.25	$36.99	$37.69
	Blake												
	Gage												
	Lowe												
	Roy												
Tag Price	$34.75												
	$36.25												
	$36.99												
	$37.69												
Percent Tax	5.5%												
	6%												
	6.5%												
	7%												

Two Pieces of Pizza

Five famished friends went out for pizza last Friday. They ordered five small pizzas, each with a different topping. The waiter did not cut each pizza exactly in half, so each friend ate + or − half of a pizza with one topping for their first slice and + or − half of a pizza with a different topping for their second slice. Find the decimal equivalencies (numerator ÷ denominator) for each slice (fractions), and write them in the chart. Round to nearest thousandths. Read the clues to find out each friend's first and second slices. Record toppings as you find them in the clues.

Clues

1. Ionia and Horton had bacon slices.
2. Bristow's and Horton's second slices were larger than their first slices.
3. The smallest first slice was pepperoni, and the smallest second slice was sausage.
4. Ackley's first slice was a mere .005 less than Denver's second slice.
5. Nobody's slices were complementary, so nobody ate exactly one whole pizza.
6. Bristow's taco slice was .005 less than Ionia's cheese slice (her smaller slice).

More Math Logic Mysteries © Prufrock Press Inc.

Two Pieces of Pizza, Continued

		First Slice					Second Slice				
topping ➤											
fraction ➤		$\frac{7}{16}$	$\frac{6}{13}$	$\frac{9}{17}$	$\frac{8}{15}$	$\frac{5}{9}$	$\frac{4}{9}$	$\frac{7}{15}$	$\frac{8}{17}$	$\frac{7}{13}$	$\frac{9}{16}$
decimal ➤				.529							
	Ackley										
	Bristow										
	Denver										
	Horton										
	Ionia										
$\frac{4}{9}$											
$\frac{7}{15}$											
$\frac{8}{17}$											
$\frac{7}{13}$											
$\frac{9}{16}$											

Algeboy Class

Mrs. Fox teaches challenge math to 13 girls and 13 boys. One small group contains all boys. Last Wednesday students were assigned three algebra problems. She showed examples and explained that n is the unknown number, and it varies from one problem to another. When there is more than one n and more than one number in a problem, they are collected together before solving.

For example:

$3n + 2 + 4n + 6 = 29$ (Collect $3n + 4n = 7n$, and collect $2 + 6 = 8$)

$7n + 8 = 29$ ($7n$ is like saying 7 times n, so $7 \times$ some number $+ 8 = 29$)

$7n + 8 - 8 = 29 - 8$ ($- 8$ from the left to make 0, but also $- 8$ from the right to balance)

$7n = 21$ (7 times $n = 21$, so $7 \times$ what number $= 21$?)

  $n = 3$ (Insert value of n $\rightarrow$ $[3 \times 3] + 2 + [4 \times 3] + 6$ is $9 + 2 + 12 + 6 = 29$)

Solve for n in each of the three problems to determine the correct answers, and then use the clues to specify which answer each boy found as he solved for n in the three problems.

Clues

1. Obid got the same answer for problems 1 and 2.
2. Zeb got the same answer for problems 2 and 3.
3. For problem 3, J.D.'s answer was larger than Obid's, but smaller than McNeal's.
4. The one who got 6 as an answer for problem 1 did not get 6 as an answer for problem 2.
5. The one who got 7 as an answer for problem 1 did not get 7 as an answer for problem 3.
6. One boy's answer on one problem was ¼ his answer on another problem.
7. Someone got all three answers correct. Who was it? _____

Algeboy Class, Continued

		Problem 1 (n =)				Problem 2 (n =)				Problem 3 (n =)			
		$2n + 6 + 3n - 1 = 35$				$4n - 3 + 3n - 2 = 23$				$5n - 6 - 3n + 5 = 13$			
		$n = 2$	$n = 3$	$n = 6$	$n = 7$	$n = 3$	$n = 4$	$n = 6$	$n = 8$	$n = 4$	$n = 5$	$n = 6$	$n = 7$
	J.D.												
	McNeal												
	Obid												
	Zeb												
Problem 3	$n = 4$												
Problem 3	$n = 5$												
Problem 3	$n = 6$												
Problem 3	$n = 7$												
Problem 2	$n = 3$												
Problem 2	$n = 4$												
Problem 2	$n = 6$												
Problem 2	$n = 8$												

Track and Field Day

Four members of the girl's track and field team are very competitive. They have comparable talent so they strive to challenge one another. At a recent meet, each competed in the long jump, discus throw, and 100-meter dash. Read the clues and find each girl's distances in the field events and place in the 100-meter dash. Complete the empty spaces in the grid by converting feet and inches to inches and yards (12" = 1 foot, 36" = 1 yard).

Clues

1. The two who threw 979" and jumped 194" were either first or fourth in the dash.
2. Dellah placed either second or fourth in the dash.
3. Kendra was neither the one who got second in the dash nor the one who threw the discus 1036".
4. The girl who jumped 5.25 yards did not get fourth in the dash, but she placed behind Sigrid and the girl who tossed the discus 26.14 yards.
5. The girl who jumped 5.14 yards also threw the discus 31.17 yards.

	long jump				discus throw				100 meter dash			
yards ➤	4.89				27.19							
inches ➤			189					1122				
	14' 8"	15' 5"	15' 9"	16' 2"	78' 5"	81' 7"	86' 4"	93' 6"	1st	2nd	3rd	4th
Aditi												
Dellah												
Kendra												
Sigrid												
1st												
2nd												
3rd												
4th												
78' 5"												
81' 7"												
86' 4"												
93' 6"												

Money for Music

Addison wanted to learn to play guitar, but he would need money for lessons, which cost $10 per half-hour lesson. Addison asked his five uncles who live nearby if they would pay him to do projects for them. Each uncle had Addison do a different task a various number of times and paid different rates for his help. Complete the table as you discover information in clues such as "paper route for 10 days." Deduce which task each uncle offered Addison, how much he paid per task, plus the total each uncle paid. How many half-hour lessons can Addison get? _____

Clues

1. The five uncles are: one who had Addison help clean the garage on two Saturdays, one who paid $20 per task, Alden, one who asked Addison to take his son's paper route for 10 days, and one who paid $5 per task.
2. Garth and the one who paid $25 per task each had Addison help twice, and Uncle Ralph requested four visits after his back surgery.
3. One Sunday, Addison and Alden sorted out used items for Goodwill.
4. Addison earned more doing his cousin's paper route than scooping snow, which paid better than pet sitting twice (which was not for Ralph).
5. Uncle Ralph paid more than Uncle Hugh who paid more than Uncle Garth did for tending his cat.

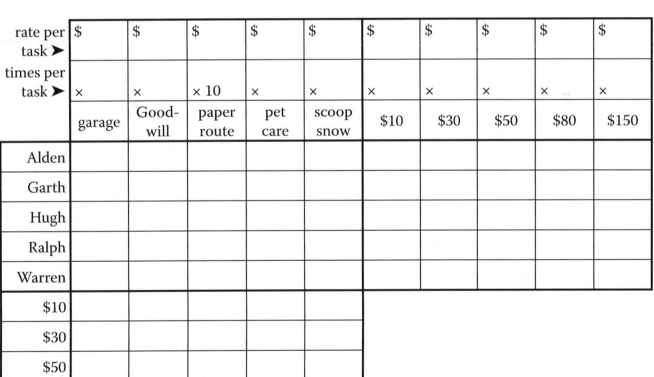

rate per task ➤	$	$	$	$	$	$	$	$	$	$
times per task ➤	×	×	× 10	×	×	×	×	×	×	×
	garage	Good-will	paper route	pet care	scoop snow	$10	$30	$50	$80	$150
Alden										
Garth										
Hugh										
Ralph										
Warren										
$10										
$30										
$50										
$80										
$150										

Water, Water Everywhere

Evergreen Exercise Club members (including two boys named Douglas and Keegan) recorded a certain day's water intake during 2 weeks. Convert cups to ounces for Week 1 and ounces to cups for Week 2 (1 c. = 8 fl. oz.) and write them in the grid. Find out which member recorded the amount they drank on which day each week. How many total ounces or cups did each member drink on his or her 2 days?

Clues

1. The one who drank 55 fl. oz. of water did not drink 8 ¾ c. on the same day the next week.
2. The person who drank 6 ½ c. of water recorded one day after Tamara and one day before the one who drank 67 fl. oz.
3. Belle recorded one day before the boy who drank 7 ⅝ c. and one day after the one who recorded drinking 62 fl. oz.
4. Douglas drank 50 fl. oz. of water during his day of week 1.
5. Douglas recorded one day after the girl who drank 7 ⅞ c. (who wasn't Jolee). The one who drank 69 fl. oz. recorded one day after the one who drank 7 ¼ c. (who wasn't Tamara).
6. Jolee recorded on Wednesdays.

Name: Date:

Water, Water Everywhere, Continued

	Day					Week 1					Week 2				
	Mon.	Tues.	Wed.	Thurs.	Fri.	6 ¼ c. fl. oz.	6 ⅞ c. fl. oz.	7 ¾ c. fl. oz.	8 ⅜ c. fl. oz.	8 ⅝ c. fl. oz.	c. 52 fl. oz.	c. 58 fl. oz.	c. 61 fl. oz.	c. 63 fl. oz.	c. 70 fl. oz.
Belle															
Douglas															
Jolee															
Keegan															
Tamara															
c. 52 fl. oz.															
c. 58 fl. oz.															
c. 61 fl. oz.															
c. 63 fl. oz.															
c. 70 fl. oz.															
6 ¼ c. fl. oz.															
6 ⅞ c. fl. oz.															
7 ¾ c. fl. oz.															
8 ⅜ c. fl. oz.															
8 ⅝ c. fl. oz.															

Down the Dogs

As a reward for increasing the number of books read during the month of March, the principal at Piedmont Prep School challenged students to play Lucky 7. The seven teams of students who ate the most pie and hot dogs in 2 minutes could skip Thursday's homework. Three of the winning teams had female captains named Jaylene, Liesa, and Suzy. Adlai, Edgar, Gerard, and Manuel led the boys' teams that were permitted to skip homework. Use the clues to discover how many hot dogs and slices of pie each team ate. (Only team captains' names are listed.)

Clues

1. No team ate the same number of pie slices as hot dogs.
2. Edgar's team ate less pie than Manuel's team.
3. Gerard's and Liesa's teams each ate a combination of nine items.
4. Adlai's team ate two fewer hot dogs than Suzy's had pie, and Liesa's team ate two fewer hot dogs than Adlai's had pie.
5. The team that devoured seven pieces of pie ate three fewer hot dogs than the team that ate five pieces of pie.
6. Adlai's team had ½ as many hot dogs as pie and Liesa's team ate ½ as much pie as hot dogs.
7. A girl captain's team ate the most hot dogs and a boy captain's team ate the fewest hot dogs.

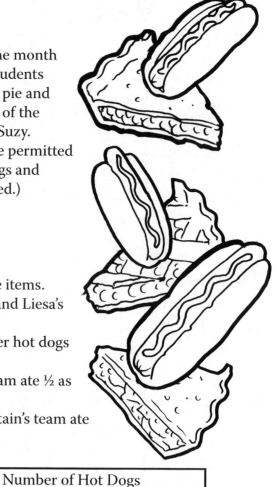

		Pieces of Pie							Number of Hot Dogs						
		2	3	5	6	7	7 ½	8	3	4	5	6	6 ½	7	8
Adlai															
Edgar															
Gerard															
Jaylene															
Liesa															
Manuel															
Suzy															
Number of Hot Dogs	3														
	4														
	5														
	6														
	6 ½														
	7														
	8														

The Pigskin

The Pigskin Restaurant serves pork dishes exclusively. Owner Roger Dodger exhibits his 6,528 NFL football cards there. He holds a monthly contest for fans to display their collections. Five July finalists exhibited their cards for patrons to vote on the most creative arrangement. Match each fan with the number of cards in his or her collection, favorite team, and how he or she ranked in the contest. Calculate percent using Roger's total. For example: 8% fewer than Roger's total cards is 6,528 × .92 (100 − .08). You will need to round your calculations to the nearest whole number. You also may need to research team mascots online to complete this puzzle (check out http://www.nfl.com for information on team mascots).

Clues
1. Faith loves the Falcons. Her display placed immediately behind the one who had 4% fewer cards than Roger.
2. The collector who has 6,079 cards earned one place higher than the one whose favorite team is the Dolphins, and one place lower than Simon who didn't have 5% fewer cards than Roger.
3. Mariah's entry earned third place, but she is not the one who has 6,205 cards.
4. The Bears fan does not have 3% fewer cards than Roger.
5. The one with 6,205 cards earned one place lower than Brock who earned one place lower than the Broncos fan.

	number of football cards					favorite football team					contest ranking				
	6,079	6,202	6,205	6,267	6,332	Atlanta	Chicago	Denver	Miami	Minnesota	1st	2nd	3rd	4th	5th
Brock															
Faith															
Mariah															
Porter															
Simon															
1st															
2nd															
3rd															
4th															
5th															
Atlanta															
Chicago															
Denver															
Miami															
Minnesota															

Making the Grade

Seven siblings (including boys Alvin, Doyle, and Lyle) entered a cookie-baking contest at school. Each is in a different grade and earned a different place for his or her cookie recipe. Use the clues to find out which child is in which grade and the place they earned for their cookies. *Note:* A small number grade is low (first is lowest) and a small number place is high (first is highest).

Clues

1. Hellen was three places higher than Doyle and two grades higher than the child who ranked two places higher than Betty.
2. The sixth grader earned eighth place.
3. Doyle (who was not in first grade) was one grade lower than the girl who earned one place lower than Lyle.
4. Lyle is three grades ahead of the child who got third place.
5. Rose is one grade higher than the child who rated one place higher than Doyle.
6. Alvin's place was one higher than the seventh grader.
7. Betty (who isn't a first grader) got one place lower than the seventh grader, who is a grade behind the second-place girl.
8. The first grader got two places higher than the sixth grader.

	Grade							Place						
	1st	2nd	3rd	5th	6th	7th	8th	1st	2nd	3rd	4th	6th	7th	8th
Alvin														
Betty														
Doyle														
Hellen														
Lyle														
Rose														
Virginia														
Place 1st														
Place 2nd														
Place 3rd														
Place 4th														
Place 6th														
Place 7th														
Place 8th														

More Math Logic Mysteries © Prufrock Press Inc.

How Many Hobbies?

Mr. Howland's fifth graders are pen pals with his fifth-grade nieces and nephews from other towns. They correspond about their unique hobbies. The nieces and two nephews (Harley and Houston) collect hamsters, harmonicas, hats, hooded sweatshirts, and horse figurines. Heed the hints and hammer out the hometowns and hobbies of Howland's handwriters. Also list the nieces and nephews in order from who has the most to the least number of items in his or her collection.

Clues

1. The girl from Hampton owns more items than the boy who likes hats, but fewer items than the girl who loves horses.
2. Hayley has more items than the one from Hazleton who owns more items than the girl who has harmonicas.
3. One left her hooded sweatshirt when visiting Holly, but it wasn't in Hudson or at the horse-lover's home.
4. Holly has more items in her collection than the boy from Huxley, but fewer items than the girl from Hazleton.
5. Houston has more items than the one who collects horses, but fewer items than the one from Hiawatha.

Most items _____ _____ _____ _____ _____ Least items

	Hampton	Hazleton	Hiawatha	Hudson	Huxley	hamsters	harmonicas	hats	hooded sweatshirts	horses
Hadlee										
Harley										
Hayley										
Holly										
Houston										
hamsters					
harmonicas					
hats					
hooded sweatshirts					
horses					

Gallons for Gals

Seven girls met at scouting camp and became good friends. Each scout was assigned a different chore that required measuring different amounts of items (foods and liquids). Write in equivalencies for cups, quarts, and gallons (4 cups = 1 quart and 4 quarts = 1 gallon) in the chart. Decipher the clues and deduce which scout did which chore and what quantity she measured out.

Clues
1. One girl used three times as many cups of water for horses as another used to make lemonade.
2. Leanne did not make food or gas the boat, but she used twice as many gallons of water as the one who washed dishes (not Natalie or Gigi).
3. The number of cups used to do laundry is a multiple of the number of cups Velvet used to make potato salad for lunch.
4. Natalie used twice as many quarts of water to clean latrines as Gigi did to prepare lemonade.
5. D'Andra used a quantity of gallons of water that is a multiple of 7, and Quasondra's water usage (in gallons) is a multiple of 6. Neither filled the boat with gas.
6. The gallons of gas used for the boat is a multiple of gallons of potato salad × water for lemonade.

chore ➤							
cups ➤	cups	112 cups	cups	224 cups	cups	384 cups	cups
quarts ➤	16 qts.	qts.	qts.	qts.	84 qts.	qts.	qts.
gallons ➤	gal.	gal.	12 gal.	gal.	gal.	gal.	28 gal.
D'Andra							
Gigi							
Leanne							
Natalie							
Quasondra							
Velvet							
Yvonne							

Solutions

The introduction, charts, and clues contain enough information to solve each puzzle. However, if you get stuck, use the descriptions in this section to figure something out. The descriptions below reflect the author's reasoning. You might use different thinking and still get correct solutions. The important thing is that you are using good logic and reasoning.

Teachers and parents may use the solutions to check student accuracy, or students may self-check their answers. Solutions are described in order of clues and step-by-step reasoning. Correct missing information for charts and other fill-in boxes is found at the beginning of the description. A summary of correct answers is at the end of the description.

Brackets such as [2] refer to something learned in Clue 2 and the denotation (only one) means there is only one empty box horizontally or vertically. Mark the empty box with O.

Let's Play Ball

Clue 1: If JoAnn is 72, half is 36; if JoAnn is 54, half is 27 (no 27); if JoAnn is 48, half is 24. So, JoAnn isn't 24, 36, or 54. You don't know who the other cousin is, so you can't mark it now.

Clue 2: ⅔ is .666 . . . , so 72 × .666 = 47.952 (round to 48), 54 × .666 = 35.964 (round to 36), 48 × .666 = 31.968 (round to 32; no 32), and 36 × .666 = 23.976 (round to 24), so Ann is 72, 54, or 36, not 24 or 48; and LaVonne is 48, 36, or 24, not 54 or 72.

Clue 3: If LeRoy is 72, LaVonne is 36; if LeRoy is 54, LaVonne is 27 (no 27); If LeRoy is 48, LaVonne is 24. So LeRoy isn't 24, 36, or 54 and LaVonne isn't 48, 54, or 72. If LaVonne can't be 48 [3], then Ann can't be 72 [2].

Clue 4: 8/9 is .888 . . . , so 72 × .888 = 63.936 (round to 64; no 64); 54 × .888 = 47.952 (round to 48); 48 × .888 = 42.624 (round to 43; no 43); 36 × .888 = 31.968 (round to 32; no 32); so Louise is 54 and LeRoy is 48 (only possibilities).

Further Reasoning: If LeRoy is 48, LaVonne is 24 [3]. If LaVonne is 24, Ann is 36 [2]; JoAnn is 72 (only one).

Answers: Ann, 36; JoAnn, 72; LaVonne, 24; LeRoy, 48; Louise, 54.

Happy Birth Date to You

Clue 1: Grant could be 2nd, 4th, 8th, or 12th, so Grant is not 10th, 16th, or 24th; Lars could be 4th, 8th, 16th, or 24th, so Lars is not 2nd, 10th, or 12th.

Clue 2: Lars isn't 2nd (Clue 1 and no 3rd), 4th (no 6th), 10th (Clue 1 and no 15th), 12th (Clue 1 and no 18th), or 24th (can't be largest), so he could be 8th or 16th; then Grant is not 12th or 2nd [1]; Valerie could be either 12th or 24th so Valerie is not 2nd, 4th, 8th, 10th, or 16th.

Clue 3: Onalee could be 4th or 8th (only ones that are ⅓ of another), so she is not 2nd, 10th, 12th, 16th, or 24th; Trey could be 12th or 24th so he is not 2nd, 4th, 8th, 10th, or 16th.

Clue 4: Fourths could be 2nd/8th or 4th/16th, but in Clue 1, Grant was eliminated from 16th, so he is 8th; he can't be 4th because Emilio would be 1 (¼ of 4), and there isn't a 1, so Emilio is 2nd and Grant is 8th. Then Bruce is 10th, Onalee is 4th, and Lars is 16th (only ones).

Further Reasoning: Going back to Clue 2, because Lars is 16th, Valerie must be 24th. In Clue 3 Onalee is 4th, so Trey must be 12th.

Answers: Bruce, 10th; Emilio, 2nd; Grant, 8th; Lars, 16th; Onalee, 4th; Trey, 12th; Valerie, 24th.

I'll Be a Bunny for Money

Clue 1: Waverly can't be 86.1 (least); 78% farther is 1.78, so try 86.1 × 1.78 = 153.26 (no); 122.84 × 1.78 = 218.66; 141.2 × 1.78 = 251.34 (no, too high), so Waverly is 218.66 m.

Clue 2: Pearl can't be 245 (most) or 218.66 [1, Waverly]; 39% less is 61% of another distance, so try .61 × 245 = 149.45 (no); .61 × 218.66 = 133.38 (no); .61 × 155.25 = 94.7025 (no); .61 × 141.2 = 86.132, so Pearl is 86.1.

Clue 3: 64% farther (1.64) than Pearl [86.1, clue 2] is 86.1 × 1.64 = 141.204 so Razi is 13% less than the one who hopped 141.2 m; 13% less is 87% of another distance, so 141.2 × .87 = 122.84 m, which is Razi's distance.

Clue 4: Kaiya is not 218.66 (Waverly is) or 122.84 (Razi is), so try the remaining possibilities: 9% less is 91% of another distance, so try .91 × 245 = 222.95 (no); .91 × 155.25 = 141.2775 (which rounds to 141.28 for hundredths); .91 × 141.2 = 128.492 (no); so Kaiya is 155.25 m.

Clue 5: 12% farther is 1.12. The only distances remaining are 141.2 and 245 m, so try 86.1 × 1.12 (12% more) = 96.432 (no); 122.84 × 1.12 = 137.58 (no); 141.2 × 1.12 = 158.144 (no); 155.25 × 1.12 = 173.88 (no); 218.66 × 1.12 = 244.8992 (round to 244.90), so Dale is 245 m and Langley must be 141.2 m.

Answers: Dale, 245 m; Kaiya, 155.25 m; Langley, 141.2 m; Pearl, 86.1 m; Razi, 122.84 m; Waverly, 218.66 m.

They Got Speed

Differences are +3, -1, 0, +2, 0, -3, +1, -2, 0.

Clue 1: Walter isn't 67 or 68 mph; Diana isn't 55 or 68 mph; Jade isn't 55 or 56 mph.

Clue 2: Phyllis isn't 56, 58, 60, 61, 65, 67, or 68; Daryl isn't 55, 58, 60, 61, 64, 67, or 68.

Clue 3: Karen isn't 55, 56, 58, 61, 64, 65, or 68; Diana isn't 55 or 68 [1], 56, 60, 64, 65, or 67; David isn't 55, 58, 60, 61, 64, 67, or 68.

Clue 4: Jade isn't a + or exact, so she isn't 55 or 56 [1], 58, 60, 61, 65, or 68; Walter isn't 67 or 68 [1], 55, 56, 60, 64, or 65.

Clue 5: Karen, Daryl, and Lisa add up to +6, so they must all be + mph guesses. Karen was 2 off [3] so she is +2 (60 mph), Daryl was 1 off [2] so he is +1 (65 mph), and Lisa must be +3 (55 mph).

Further Reasoning: Mark is 68 mph (only one); Phyllis is -3 [2] (64 mph) because +3 is Lisa; Jade is -2 [4] (67 mph) and David is -1 [3] (56 mph; only ones). Walter's car was slower than Diana's [1], so he is 58 mph and Diana is 61 mph.

79

Answers: Daryl, 65; David, 56; Diana, 61; Jade, 67; Karen, 60; Lisa, 55; Mark, 68; Phyllis, 64; Walter, 58.

September Sleepover

Totals costs: $17.19 for apples ($8.16) and cookies ($9.03); $17.50 for DVD rental; $17.47 for beverages ($5.40 for sodas, $7.08 for water, $4.99 for juice); $17.29 for veggies ($11.62) and dips ($5.67); $17.46 for decorations and napkins; $17.54 chips ($12.76) and salsas ($4.78).

Notice in the introduction, alphabetically, Aleasha isn't apples (and cookies); Bethany isn't beverages; Chelsea isn't chips (and salsa) or cookies (and apples); Dixie isn't dips (and veggies), decorations (and napkins), or DVD rentals; Nicole isn't napkins (and decorations); Vanessa isn't veggies (and dips).

Clue 1: Aleasha isn't $17.54, Bethany isn't $17.19. Refer back to this clue later.

Clue 2: $17.19 is 2% less than $17.54. Dixie isn't $17.19.

Clue 3: Aleasha and Vanessa aren't beverages ($17.47).

Clue 4: Dixie is $17.54 or $17.50 and Bethany is $17.50 or $17.46, but Dixie isn't $17.50 (DVDs) because they both start with D, so Dixie is $17.54 and Bethany is $17.50.

Clue 5: Nicole isn't $17.19 (Chelsea spent less). Chelsea can't be $17.47 because she spent less than at least three girls (Nicole, Dixie, and Bethany). Then Nicole is $17.47 and Vanessa is $17.19 (only ones).

Further Reasoning: In Clue 1, Aleasha is less than $.20 from Bethany's total; $17.29 is a difference of $.21 (too much) and Aleasha isn't $17.19 [both start with "a", Intro.], so she spent $17.46 (difference of $.04). Chelsea is $17.29 (only one).

Answers: Aleasha, $17.46; Bethany, $17.50; Chelsea, $17.29; Dixie, $17.54; Nicole, $17.47; Vanessa, $17.19. The girls spent $104.45 and the parents spent $36 on pizza, so the party cost $140.45.

Newton's Newbies

Clue 1: Mariposa isn't 1 week; Holbrook isn't 11 weeks.

Clue 2: Carlotta isn't 11 weeks; Sagar isn't 1 week.

Clue 3: Mariposa isn't 11 weeks; Carlotta isn't 1 week or 2 weeks (the least Mariposa could be because she isn't 1 week [1]); Mariposa can't be 9 weeks (the most Carlotta could be because she isn't 11 weeks [2]).

Clue 4: Sagar came 2 weeks after Jamee, so Jamee has been there longer. The only ones with a difference of 2 weeks are 9 and 11, so Jamee is 11 weeks and Sagar is 9 weeks.

Clue 5: Holbrook isn't 1 week, so Garrison is 1 week (only one). Combine clues 1, 3, and 5 to see that Carlotta is longer than Mariposa who is longer than Holbrook who is longer than Garrison; Carlotta is 6 weeks, Mariposa is 5 weeks; Holbrook is 2 weeks.

Answers: Carlotta, 6 weeks; Garrison, 1 week; Holbrook, 2 weeks; Jamee, 11 weeks; Mariposa, 5 weeks; Sagar, 9 weeks.

Tri This Problem on for Size

Chart: Monday—6 sq. in., 10 sq. in., 31.5 sq. in., 44 sq. in.; Friday—28.69 sq. in.; 39.98 sq. in.; 57.95 sq. in.; 68.15 sq. in. (¾ is .75, ½ is .5, ⅘ is .8, ¼ is .25, ⅕ is .2, ⅖ is .4 for decimal equivalencies).

Clue 1: Harmony got 68.15 sq. in. on Friday.

Clue 2: Carrington got 6 sq. in. on Monday. Carrington isn't 68.15 sq. in., so 6 sq. in. doesn't go with 68.15 sq. in. [1].

Clue 3: 7 in. × 9 in. (31.5 sq. in.) on Monday isn't 28.69 sq. in. on Friday.

Clue 4: Wahneta is 57.95 sq. in. on Friday; she is not 8 in. × 11 in. (44 sq. in.) on Monday, so 44 sq. in. is not with 57.95 sq. in. and she isn't 6 sq. in. [Carrington, 2], so 57.95 sq. in. isn't with 6 sq. in.

Clue 5: 39.98 sq. in. is nearly 40 sq. in., so it is with 10 sq. in. on Monday (4 in. × 5 in.). Carrington isn't 10 sq. in. [2], so he isn't 39.98 sq. in.; he's 28.69 sq. in. on Friday, which is with 6 sq. in. Monday. Tripp is 39.98 sq. in. (only one) so he is also 10 sq. in. Harmony is 44 sq. in. on Monday (only one), which is with 68.15 sq. in on Friday [1]. Wahneta is 31.5 sq. in. on Monday (only one), which is with 57.95 sq. in. on Fri. [4].

Answers: Carrington, 6 sq. in., 28.69 sq. in.; Harmony, 44 sq. in., 68.15 sq. in.; Tripp, 10 sq. in., 39.98 sq. in.; Wahneta, 31.5 sq. in., 57.95 sq. in.

Piles of Pencils and Scores of Sports Cards

Clue 1: The only combination that works is 16 × 11 = 176, so Dante has 16 pencils; Clay has 176 cards; Clay doesn't have 16 pencils.

Clue 2: Oliana doesn't have 24 pencils.

Clue 3: The only combination that works is ⅓ of 24 = 8, so Mamiko has 8 pencils and Clay has 24, which is with 176 cards [1].

Clue 4: 8 × 12 = 96 and 16 × 12 = 192, so either Mamiko has 8 pencils [3] and 96 cards or Dante has 16 pencils [1] and 192 cards. Refer back to this clue later.

Clue 5: Tanner is 13, 21, or 32 pencils (others already marked "yes"). Then 9 × 13 = 117, 9 × 21 = 189 (no), and 9 × 32 = 288 (no), so Tanner has 13 pencils; the one with 21 pencils has 117 cards, and Tanner doesn't have 117 cards; 21 pencils isn't Clay [3], Dante [1], Mamiko [4], or Tanner, so 117 cards isn't Clay, Dante, Mamiko, or Tanner.

Clue 6: 192 cards isn't with 13 pencils, so Tanner isn't 192 cards.

Clue 7: Oliana is 21 or 32 pencils (others already marked "yes"). Then 7 × 21 = 147 and 7 × 32 = 224 (no), so Tanner has 147 cards, which is with 13 pencils; Oliana has 21 pencils, which was with 117 cards, so Oliana has 117 cards. Erika has 32 pencils (only one).

Clue 8: 205 − 192 is the only difference of 13, so Dante has 205 cards; Erika has 192 cards; and Mamiko has 96 cards (only one), so she is the one from clue 4 who has 12 times as many cards as pencils. Dante had 16 pencils [1]. Erika has 32 pencils [7], which is with 192 cards, and 16 pencils [Dante, 1] is with 205 cards.

Answers: Clay, 24 pencils, 176 cards; Dante, 16 pencils, 205 cards; Erika, 32 pencils, 192 cards; Mamiko, 8 pencils, 96 cards; Oliana, 21 pencils, 117 cards; Tanner, 13 pencils, 147 cards.

Can You Hear Me Now?

Clue 1: 5.1 × 2.3 × .9 in. is with 240 × 160 pixels.

Clue 2: Nokia is 87 × 78 × 19 mm; Nokia isn't 5.1 × 2.3 × .9 in., so it isn't 240 × 160 pixels [1].

Clue 3: The 7-oz. phone is 5.1 × 2.3 × .9 in., so it is also 240 × 160 pixels [1]; Nokia is 87 × 78 × 19 mm [2], so it isn't 7 oz.

Clue 4: BlackBerry is 320 × 240 pixels; Nokia is 128 × 160 pixels; Sidekick˚ 3 is 240 × 160 pixels (only ones). Sidekick˚ 3 is 7 oz. and 5.1 × 2.3 × .9 in., because 240 × 160 pixels goes with 7 oz. and 5.1 × 2.3 × .9 in. [3]; 87 × 78 × 19 mm is with 128 × 160 pixels (both go with Nokia); 50 × 106.7 × 14.5 mm is with 320 × 240 pixels (only one). The BlackBerry is 50 × 106.7 × 14.5 mm (only one).

Clue 5: 128 × 160 pixels is with 123 grams, so 320 × 240 pixels is with 87.9 grams (only one). Nokia is 128 × 160 pixels, so it weighs 123 grams (only one). The BlackBerry weighs 87.9 grams.

Answers: BlackBerry, 50 × 106.7 × 14.5 mm, 320 × 240 pixels, 87.9 g; Nokia 7600, 87 × 78 × 19 mm, 128 × 160 pixels, 123 grams; Sidekick˚ 3, 5.1 × 2.3 × .9 in., 240 × 160 pixels, 7 oz.

Meow Mixer

Clue 1: Brady isn't ½ c or ⅝ c. of food.

Clue 2: Brady and Roscoe aren't $7.98.

Clue 3: ⅝ c. isn't $8.69 or $9.40.

Clue 4: Roscoe's food isn't $10.11 and Jiffy's food isn't $7.98. Then Daisy's food costs $7.98 (only one).

Clue 5: Brady's food isn't $10.11, so Jiffy's is $10.11 (only one). Brady doesn't eat ¾ cup because his food costs less than the one who eats ¾ cup. Then, Brady eats ⅞ cup (only one), which isn't $7.98 or $10.11 (not Brady's costs). Brady's food costs less than the other cats, so Brady is not $10.11, Jiffy is $10.11 (only one).

Clue 6: ⅞ − ¼ (²⁄₈) = ⅝ cup. Jiffy eats ⅝ cup of food.

Further Reasoning: Roscoe doesn't eat ½ cup of food because his owner is Winifred, and Spencer's cat is the one that eats ½ cup. So, Daisy eats ½ cup and Roscoe eats ¾ cup (only ones). Daisy's food costs $7.98, so ½ cup is with $7.98. Brady's food is $8.69 or $9.40. The one who eats ¾ cup is $8.69 or $9.40. But, Brady's food costs less [5], so Brady is $8.69 (⅞ cup) and ¾ cup (Roscoe) goes with $9.40.

Answers: Brady, ⅞ cup, $8.69; Daisy, ½ cup, $7.98; Jiffy, ⅝ cup, $10.11; Roscoe, ¾ cup, $9.40.

American Girls

Clue 1: Possibilities are Freedom = Flippy, Independence = Itchy, Starr = Scruffy.

Clue 2: Starr is 30,390; 40,250; or 60,780, so she isn't 15,195 or 20,260; Flippy is 15,195; 20,260; or 30,390, so she isn't 40,250 or 60,780; and Starr is not Flippy.

Clue 3: Americus is 15,195; 20,260; or 30,390; Liberty is 30,390; 40,250; or 60,780.

Clue 4: Scruffy is 15,195. Liberty and Starr are not Scruffy (not 15,195).

Clue 5: 15,195 is ¼ of 60,780, so Starr is 60,780 and Independence is 15,195. Independence is Scruffy [4].

Clue 6: Americus is 20,260 or 30,390 and Itchy is 20,260 or 40,520 (can't be the largest score). The only equation possible is 20,260 + 40,520 = 60,780, so Mushy is 60,780; Starr is Mushy [5].

Further Reasoning: Americus is not 40,520 [3], so she is 20,620. Americus is ½ of Liberty [3], so Liberty is 40,520; Itchy

is 40,520, so Itchy is Liberty. Freedom is 30,390. Refer to Clue 1. Independence isn't Itchy ("I" names) and Starr isn't Scruffy ("S" names), so Freedom is Flippy (both "F" names). Chilly is Americus (only one).

Answers: Americus, 20,260, Chilly; Freedom, 30,390, Flippy; Independence, 15,195, Scruffy; Liberty, 40,520, Itchy; Starr, 60,780, Mushy.

Saddle Up

Clue 1: Denny is not June or July; Judy is not March or July; Lila is not March or April. Judy is not bridling or saddling.

Clue 2: Trudy is not May, June, or July; Bobby is not March, April, or May. Trudy is not bridling or leading; Bobby is not bridling or leading.

Clue 3: Shoeing is not March, April, or July; Denny is not May; Lila is not May. Then Judy is May (only one), so May is not bridling or saddling [1]. Lila is not roping or shoeing; Denny is not roping or shoeing.

Clue 4: Bobby is not roping or shoeing, he's saddling (only one). Bridling is one month after shoeing and one month before Bobby. Then bridling is June and Bobby is July. Shoeing is May (only one). Judy is May [3], so Judy is shoeing.

Further Reasoning: Lila is June (only one) and bridling (which is June). Trudy is roping (only one). Leading is Denny (only one). Bobby is July, so Trudy is April [2]. Denny is March [3 and only one].

Answers: Bobby, saddling, July; Denny, leading, March; Judy, shoeing, May; Lila, bridling, June; Trudy, roping, April.

Gee, It's Great to Be a Newsboy (or Girl!)

Clue 1: Wagon is a boy (not Flora or Fauna) or Hunter (wagon is before Hunter). Wagon isn't Friday or Saturday (two are after wagon). Hunter is not Tuesday or Saturday (one is before and one is after him). Fauna is not Tuesday or Wednesday (two are before her).

Clue 2: Cart is not Saturday. Moped is not Tuesday.

Clue 3: Walk is a girl (not Fisher, Hunter, or Trapper). Walking is not Tuesday, Wednesday, or Saturday (two before, one after). Bicycle is not Thursday, Friday, or Saturday (three are after). Trapper is not Tuesday, Wednesday, or Thursday (three before); Trapper is not bicycle or walking. Moped is Saturday (only one). Hunter is not Saturday, so he is not moped.

Clue 4: Fauna does not walk. A girl walks [3], so Flora walks. She does not deliver Tuesday, Wednesday, or Saturday [3], she delivers Thursday or Friday.

Further Reasoning: Flora delivers one day after Fauna, who does not deliver on Wednesday [1], so Flora is Friday, Fauna is Thursday, and Trapper is Saturday. The moped is Saturday [3], so Trapper drives a moped. Hunter is Wednesday and Fisher is Tuesday (only ones). The walker (Flora) is 2 days after the biker, so Hunter is the biker. Fauna uses the cart (only one).

Answers: Fauna, Thursday, cart; Fisher, Tuesday, wagon; Flora, Friday, walking; Hunter, Wednesday, bicycle; Trapper, Saturday, moped.

The Guys' Cash Stash

Clue 1: P.J. is $88.62 or $37.38. Mason is $29.54 or $12.46. P.J. is not Mason.

Clue 2: Basil is not Carson.

Clue 3: Howie is $37.38 or $29.54. Basil is $29.54 or $12.46. O'Banyon is $88.62 or $37.38. Howie and Basil are not O'Banyon.

Clue 4: Carson is $88.62 or $37.38. Fereday is $29.54 or $12.46.

Clue 5: O'Banyon is $88.62 or $37.38, so Howie would be $29.54 or $12.46, but he isn't $12.46 [3], he is $29.54 and O'Banyon must be $88.62. Carson is $37.38 (only one), then Fereday is $12.46 [4]. Mason is $29.54 and Basil is $12.46 (only ones), then P.J. is $88.62 [1] and Edward is $37.38 (only one). Basil is Fereday, Edward is Carson, Howie is Mason, P.J. is O'Banyon.

Answers: Basil Fereday, $12.46; Edward Carson, $37.38; Howie Mason, $29.54; P.J. O'Banyon, $88.62. The total for 5 balls was $168, so each ball cost $33.60.

Family Reunion

Totals: $6.45 for toilet paper and $34.90 for games = $41.35; $34.68 for cookies and $6.72 for kites = $41.40; $5.34 for cards and $37.45 for sodas = $42.79; $3.78 for bubbles and $37.35 for snack cakes = $41.13; $25.65 for pretzels and $15.92 for lemonade = $41.57.

Clue 1: Friday is bubbles/cakes ($41.13).

Clue 2: Celina is Monday; Celina is not $42.79 (cards/sodas); $42.79 (cards/sodas) is not Monday. Celina is not $41.13 (bubbles/cakes) [1, Friday].

Clue 3: Wednesday is games/toilet paper ($41.35). Celina is not games/toilet paper ($41.35) [3, Monday].

Clue 4: Skyler spent $41.40 (cookies/kites); Celina is $41.57 (pretzels/lemonade; only one) and $41.57 (pretzels/lemonade) is Monday [2]. $41.40 is not Monday, Wednesday, or Friday, so Skyler isn't Monday, Wednesday, or Friday. Kara is a day ahead of him, and she isn't Monday [Celina, 2], so he can't be Tuesday. He is Thursday (only one) and Kara is Wednesday; then Thursday is also $41.40 (cookies/kites), Kara is toilet paper and games ($41.35), and $42.79 (cards/sodas) is Tuesday (only one).

Clue 5: Sophie isn't $41.13 (bubbles/cakes), so she spent $41.79 on cards/sodas which leaves Hannah for $41.13 (bubbles/cakes). Then Hannah is Friday [1], and Sophie is Tuesday, which also is $42.79.

Answers: Celina, $41.57, Monday; Hannah, $41.13, Friday; Kara, $41.35, Wednesday; Skyler, $41.40, Thursday; Sophie, $42.79, Tuesday.

Math for Moms and Dads

Clue 1: Ryne is not the seamstress. Ryne did not speak Dec. 12. The seamstress did not speak Oct. 3. George and Judd are not the seamstress (it is a feminine term, a male in this profession is called a tailor).

Clue 2: Neither Ellen nor George is the banker or the computer programmer. Ellen spoke before two people and after one, so she did not speak Oct. 3, Nov. 28, or Dec. 12. George spoke before Ellen and two others, so he did not speak Nov. 14, Nov. 28, or Dec. 12. The banker and computer programmer did not speak Oct. 3 or 21 (two spoke before them, Ellen and George).

Clue 3: Nyla and Ellen are the banker and seamstress. Ellen is not the banker [2], so she is the seamstress and Nyla is the banker. Ellen (the seamstress) did not speak Oct. 3, Nov. 28., or Dec. 12. Nyla did not speak Oct. 3 or Oct. 21 [2].

Clue 4: George is not the graphic artist or clerk. He is the carpet layer (only one). The carpet layer did not speak Nov. 14 or 28 or Dec. 12. The graphic artist spoke after one person, but before another, so he or she did not speak Oct. 3 or Dec. 12. The clerk spoke after two others (George and graphic artist), so he or she did not speak Oct. 3 or 21. The carpet layer spoke Oct. 3 (only one), so George spoke Oct. 3.

Clue 5: Judd is the clerk. Judd (the clerk) did not speak Oct. 3 (carpet layer), Oct. 21, or Nov. 1 (after graphic artist and Mrs. Walton) [4]. You don't know who Mrs. Walton is, but she spoke after the carpet layer and graphic artist and before Judd. The graphic artist did not speak Nov. 28 (two spoke after him or her).

Clue 6: Judd, the clerk, spoke 4 weeks before Carla. Dec. 12 is the only date 4 weeks after another (Nov. 14), therefore Carla spoke Dec. 12 and Judd spoke Nov. 14. Carla is not the banker, carpet layer, clerk, or seamstress, all of whom did not speak Dec. 12. The graphic artist did not speak Dec. 12 (Carla's date), so Carla is the computer programmer, and Ryne is the graphic artist (only one).

Further Reasoning: Ryne (the graphic artist) spoke after the carpet layer (Oct. 3) before the seamstress, who spoke before the banker and computer programmer [2]. The graphic artist also spoke before the clerk. Ryne spoke before three others, so Ryne spoke Oct. 21. Ellen (seamstress) spoke Nov. 1 (only one) and Nyla (banker) spoke Nov. 28 (only one).

Answers: Carla, Dec. 12, computer programmer; Ellen, Nov. 1, seamstress; George, Oct. 3, carpet layer; Judd, Nov. 14, clerk; Nyla, Nov. 28, banker; Ryne, Oct. 21, graphic artist.

Am I In the Right Area?

Areas: largest = 144.56 sq. cm., middle = 83.42 sq. cm., smallest = 74.34 sq. cm.

Clue 1: 139.56 is with 70.9, but not 80.2, so 70.9 is not with 80.2.

Clue 2: Lin isn't 139.56 or 87.5, but 139.56 is with 87.5. Then 70.9 is with 87.5 and Lin isn't with 70.9.

Clue 3: 141.3 is with 72.42. Neither is with 72.1. Then 133.6 is with 80.2 and 72.1 (only ones), and 68.4 is with 141.3 and 72.42 (only ones).

Clue 4: Kaneisha is 80.2, and 80.2 is with 72.1, so Kaneisha is 72.1. Then Geoffrey is 70.9 and 87.5 (only ones); Lin is 68.4 and 72.42 (only ones). Kaneisha is not 139.56, so Geoffrey is (only one). Lin's team is 72.42, so also 141.3 [3]; Kaneisha's is 133.6 (only one).

Answers: Geoffrey, 139.56 sq. cm, 87.5 sq. cm, 70.9 sq. cm; Kaneisha, 133.6 sq. cm, 80.2 sq. cm, 72.1 sq. cm; Lin, 141.3 sq. cm, 72.42 sq. cm, 68.4 sq. cm. Lin's team was closest on the largest rectangle; Kaneisha's team was closest on the middle and smallest rectangles.

Teaspoon Trivia

Grams of sugar: 14.31, 23.85, 33.39, 38.16;

Grams of fertilizer: 52.47, 71.55, 85.86, 109.71;

Grams of detergent: 114.48; 143.1; 171.72; 200.34.

Clue 1: Nettie isn't 71.55 g or 114.48 g and 71.55 g isn't with 114.48 g.

Clue 2: 171.72 g isn't with 85.86 g, 171.72 g isn't with 14.31 g, and 85.86 g isn't with 14.31 g.

Clue 3: Soledad isn't 14.31 g, 52.47 g, or 143.1 g; 14.31 g isn't with 52.47 g or 143.1 g; and 52.47 g isn't with 143.1 g.

Clue 4: 33.39 g isn't with 52.47 g.

Clue 5: Graham isn't 52.47 g or 109.71 g; Soledad isn't 52.47 g or 109.71 g. Because you know Graham and Soledad are 71.55 g and 85.86 g, then Farrah and Nettie can't be 71.55 g and 85.86 g. Farrah isn't 114.48 g or 200.34 g; Nettie isn't 114.48 g or 200.34 g. Because you know Farrah and Nettie are 143.1 g and 171.72 g, then Graham and Soledad can't be 143.1 g and 171.72 g.

Clue 6: Nettie is 38.16 g or 33.39 g, so isn't 14.31 g or 23.85 g; Farrah is 33.39 g or 23.85 g, so she isn't 14.31 g or 38.16 g; Soledad is 14.31 g or 23.85 g, so isn't 38.16 g or 33.39 g; Graham is 14.31 g (only one). Because Soledad is less than Nettie and Farrah, she is 23.85 g (only ones), Farrah is 33.39 g, and Nettie is 38.16 g.

Further Reasoning: Graham is 14.31 g sugar, so he is not 143.1 or 171.72 g detergent [2, 3] or 52.47 g or 85.86 g fertilizer [2, 3]. Graham and 14.31 go with 71.55 g fertilizer (only one). 71.55 does not go with 114.48 [1], so Graham does not go with 114.48. Graham is 200.34 (only one). Soledad is 114.48 (only one). If Graham used 71.55 g fertilizer, then Soledad used 85.86 g fertilizer [5, Graham and Soledad used ½ of Nettie and Farrah's amounts, and only one]. Farrah (who measured 33.39 g sugar) could not have 52.47 g fertilizer [4]. Therefore, she measured 109.71 g fertilizer and Nettie measured 52.47 g fertilizer (only ones). The person who measured 52.47 g fertilizer did not have 143.1 g detergent, so Nettie had 171.72 g detergent and Farrah had 143.1 g detergent (only ones).

Answers: Farrah, 33.39 g (7 tsp), 109.71 g (23 tsp), 143.1 g (30 tsp); Graham, 14.31 g (3 tsp), 71.55 g (15 tsp), 200.34 g (42 tsp); Nettie, 38.16 g (8 tsp), 52.47 g (11 tsp), 171.72 g (36 tsp); Soledad, 23.85 g (5 tsp), 85.86 g (18 tsp), 114.48 g (24 tsp).

This Fits Me to a T

Clue 1: Lucky #36 is a multiple of 9, which goes with #2 jersey.

Clue 2: Tabitha is not #13 jersey or #21 locker (odd numbers).

Clue 3: There are 12 sides on dodecahedrons. If she doesn't like dodecahedrons, you can assume she would not want the #12 for her lucky number; #13 (traditionally considered unlucky) jersey would not go with #12 for a lucky number. Then #10 jersey goes with lucky #12 and #13 jersey goes with lucky #24 (only ones). Tabitha is not #13 jersey, so she's not lucky #24.

Clue 4: Tonya's lucky number is 24 (only multiple of 8). Tonya has jersey #13 [3]. She isn't locker #36 (not a multiple of 7), so jersey #13 and lucky #24 don't go with locker #36.

Clue 5: Jersey #2 (divisor of 10) goes with locker #36 (multiple of 9) and also goes with lucky #36, so locker #36 goes with lucky #36.

Clue 6: Terisah isn't 21 or 28 (multiples of 7), so she is locker #36, jersey #2 [5], and lucky #36 [5]. Tabitha is lucky #12, jersey #10, and locker #28 (only ones). Tonya is locker #21 (only one).

Answers: Tabitha, #12, #10, #28; Terisah, #36, #2, #36; Tonya, #24, #13, #21.

The Great Chili Cook-Off

Cups	⅜	¾	1 ¼	1 ¾	1 ⅞	2 ¼
Oz.	3	6	10	14	15	18
Tbsp	6	12	20	28	30	36

Clue 1: Juanita is not ⅜ c.; R&B is not 2 ¼ c.; Juanita is not R&B.

Clue 2: Zylo is not ⅜ c.; reggae is not 2 ¼ c.; Zylo is not reggae.

Clue 3: 30 Tbsp is not R&B or Faresse; R&B is not Faresse, 36 Tbsp [1, most], 30 Tbsp, or 6 Tbsp (least); Faresse is not 36, 30, or 28 Tbsp (less than at least two others that are both less than 36 Tbsp).

Clue 4: Viann is not 3, 6, or 10 oz. (three less), classical or rock; classical is not 3, 6, or 18 oz. or Greta; Greta is not rock, 15 or 18 oz. (two teams use more); rock isn't 15 or 18 oz. (two teams use more).

Clue 5: Kenny Chesney's genre is country, so it is 3 oz., and Juanita is 15 oz. (only one that is ⅕ of another). 3 oz. isn't Juanita, Viann, or Zylo, so country isn't Juanita, Viann, or Zylo; 15 oz. isn't rock, so Juanita isn't rock. Hip-hop is 18 oz. (only one), which isn't Faresse, Greta, or Juanita, so hip-hop isn't Faresse, Greta, or Juanita. Rock is not 15 oz., so Juanita is not rock.

Clue 6: Faresse is 1 ¼ c., reggae is ¾ c. and Greta is ⅜ c. [and country]; no other differences work.

Further Reasoning: Classical is 15 oz. (only one) and Juanita [5]; and 10 oz. is not classical, country, hip-hop, or reggae. Faresse is 10 oz., so Faresse is not classical, country, hip hop, or reggae, and she is not R & B [3]—she's rock (only one) and 10 oz. is rock; R& B is 14 oz. (only one). Because classical is 30 Tbsp, and Viann is more than that [4], Viann is 36 Tbsp (2 ¼ c., 18 oz.) and hip-hop. Greta (6 Tbsp) + rock (20 Tbsp) = 26 Tbsp. (less than classical). Then Zylo is 14 oz. (only one) and R & B. Reggae is 12 oz. and Oscar is 12 oz. (only one), so Oscar is reggae.

Answers: Faresse, 20 T (10 oz., 1 ¼ c.), rock; Greta, 6 Tbsp (3 oz., ⅜ c.), country; Juanita, 30 Tbsp (15 oz., 1 ⅞ c.), classical; Oscar, 12 Tbsp (6 oz., ¾ c.), reggae; Viann, 36 Tbsp (18 oz., 2 ¼ c.), hip-hop; Zylo, 28 Tbsp (14 oz., 1 ¾ c.), R & B.

Stop and Smell the Roses

Clue 1: Half of $52.38 is $26.19 (no); ½ of $36.98 is $18.49 (no); ½ of $34.92 is $17.46, so Sonya spent $34.92 on Father's Day. Tabby is $17.46 on Valentine's Day (clue says "her").

Clue 2: $65.52/3 = $21.84 (no), $49.14/3 = $16.38 (yes), $18.49/3 = $6.16 (no), so Clark spent $49.14 on Mother's Day and Sonja spent $16.38 on Valentine's Day. Clark spent $65.96 on Valentine's Day (only one).

Clue 3: We know two of Clark's expenditures: $49.14/2 = $24.57 (no) and $65.96/2 = $32.98 (no). So, Tabby's spending must be half of whatever Clark spent on Father's Day: $36.98/2 = $18.49 (yes), $52.38/2 = $26.19 (no). Therefore, Clark spent $36.98 on Father's Day and Tabby spent $18.49 on Mother's Day. That means Tabby spent $52.38 on Father's Day (only one) and Sonya spent $65.52 on Mother's Day (only one).

Answers: Clark, $65.96 VD, $49.14 MD, $36.98 FD = $152.08; Sonya, $16.38 VD, $65.52 MD, $34.92 FD = $116.82; Tabby, $17.46 VD, $18.49 MD, $52.38 FD = $88.33, so Clark spent the most.

What's Your E.T.A.?

Clue 1: Jacy did not depart at 6:51 a.m. or 9:18 a.m.; 2:47 p.m. arrival isn't 6:51 a.m. or 9:18 a.m. departure; Catava did not depart at 12:03 a.m. or 5:24 a.m.; Jacy and Catava did not arrive at 2:47 p.m.

Clue 2: 5:24 a.m. departure is not with 1:59 p.m. arrival.

Clue 3: The only ones with a difference of 13 hours are Manning departing at 5:24 a.m. and Catava arriving at 6:25 p.m. 6:25 p.m. arrival is not 12:03 a.m. or 5:24 a.m. departure. Manning is not 1:59 p.m. arrival, because 5:24 a.m. departure does not go with 1:59 p.m. arrival [2].

Clue 4: Manning arrived later and earlier than someone, therefore Manning did not arrive at 8:04 a.m. or 6:25 p.m. Therefore, Manning arrived at 2:47 p.m. (only one). If Manning arrived later than the one departing at 9:18 a.m., then the 9:18 a.m. departure did not arrive at 2:47 p.m. or 6:25 p.m. 6:25 p.m. departed at 6:51 a.m. (only one), so Catava departed at 6:51 a.m. Therefore, Sutton departed at 9:18 a.m. (only one). Jacy departed at 12:03 a.m. (only one).

Clue 5: Jacy (who departed at 12:03 a.m.) did not arrive at 1:59 p.m. Jacy arrived at 8:04 a.m. and Sutton arrived at 1:59 p.m.

Answers: Catava, 6:51 a.m. depart, 6:25 p.m. arrive (11h 34 m); Jacy 12:03 a.m. depart, 8:04 a.m. arrive (8h 1m); Manning 5:24 a.m. depart, 2:47 p.m. arrive (9 h 23m); Sutton, 9:18 a.m. depart, 1:59 p.m. arrive (4h 41m); Sutton's trip was the shortest, and Catava's trip was the longest.

Sunny Side Up

Chart for Fahrenheit: 90°, 91°, 92°, 94°, 96°, 98°, 100°.

Clue 1: Thatcher isn't 90° or 91°; Fujita isn't 90° or 100°; Courtney isn't 98° or 100°.

Clue 2: Bolton isn't 91°, 92°, 94°, 98°, or 100°. He is either 15 or 16 years old.

Clue 3: Kipp isn't 90°, 92°, 94°, 96°, or 100°. He is either 13 or 14 years old.

Clue 4: Jayvyn isn't 96°, 98°, or 100°; LaRae isn't 90°, 98°, or 100° [Thatcher is 100°, only one]; Bolton and Kipp aren't 90° or 91°. Bolton is 96° and Kipp is 98° (only ones).

Clue 5: 90° and 100° are divisible by 5, but Jayvyn isn't 100° [4], so he is 90°.

Clue 6: LaRae is 92°. Fujita's day was hotter than Courtney's day, so she is 94° and Courtney is 91°.

Answers: Bolton, 96°; Courtney, 91°; Fujita, 94°; Jayvyn, 90°; Kipp, 98°; LaRae, 92°; Thatcher, 100°.

Vital Statistics

Clue 1: Rishab is 109 lbs.

Clue 2: Elina is not 116 lbs. Devitri, Kavi, and Rishab are not 116 lbs (a girl is). Elina is not 4' 6". 116 lbs is not 5' 9".

Clue 3: Devitri isn't 145 lbs, 4' 11", or 4' 6". Elina, Avaia, and Chaitra are not 145 lbs (a boy is). Kavi is 145 lbs (only one). Kavi is neither 4' 6" nor 4' 11". 145 lbs. is not with 4' 6" or 4' 11" tall. 145 lbs. is not with 4' 6" or 4' 11" tall.

Clue 4: Rishab is not 5' 1", 5' 5", or 5' 9" (three are taller than him). Chaitra is not 4' 6" (at least one shorter than her), and not 5' 5" or 5' 9" (two are taller). Neither Rishab, Chaitra, or Elina weight 134 lbs. 134 lbs is a girl, so it is not Devitri, it's Avaia (only one). Chaitra weighs 116 lbs (only one). Neither Avaia nor Elina are 4' 6" or 4' 8" tall (two are shorter than them). Rishab is 4' 6" (only one). 4' 6" is with 109 lbs. [1], so Rishab is 109 lbs.

Clue 5: A boy weighs 123 lbs. Elina does not weigh 123, Devitri does (only one). Elina weighs 118 lbs (only one). Devitri is 2" taller than Elina. The only possibilities are 4' 6" and 4' 8" and 4' 11" and 5' 1". Rishab is 4' 6", not Elina [4], so she must be 4' 11" and Devitri is 5' 1". Chaitra is 4' 8" (only one). 4' 11" is with 118 lbs. and 5' 11" is with 123 lbs.

Clue 6: Avaia is taller than Kavi, so he is 5' 5" and Avaia is 5' 9".

Answers: Avaia, 5' 9", 134 lbs; Chaitra, 4' 8", 116 lbs; Devitri, 5' 1", 123 lbs; Elina, 4' 11", 118 lbs; Kavi, 5' 5", 145 lbs; Rishab, 4' 6", 109 lbs.

Fraction Action

Equivalents: $4/15$ = .267; $7/26$ = .269; $9/33$ = .273; $11/40$ = .275; $8/29$ = .276; $13/47$ = .277; $5/18$ = .278.

Clue 1: Isabel isn't .267, .273, or .276 and Fritz isn't .269, .277, or .278.

Clue 2: Craig isn't .267 or .269, Kathleen isn't .267 or .278, and Isabel isn't .277 or .278. Then Fritz isn't .276 or .275 [1].

Clue 3: Marjorie isn't .269 or .277.

Clue 4: Isabel isn't .267 or .275, so she's .269 and Fritz is .267 [1]. Marjorie isn't .267 or .275.

Clue 5: Luther isn't .267 or .269 (already marked), Craig isn't .267 or .278, and Marjorie isn't .277 or .278. Craig also can't be .273 because his number is larger than at least three others: Kathleen's and Isabel's [2] and Marjorie's [5].

Clue 6: Grace isn't .267 [Fritz], .269 [Isabel], .273 (no .271), or .276 (no .274); and Kathleen isn't .267 [Fritz], .269 [Isabel], or .277.

Clue 7: $5/18$ is .278 and $8/29$ is .276, so Grace must be .277 and Kathleen is .275 [6]. Then Luther is .278, Craig is .276, and Marjorie is .273 (only ones).

Answers: Craig, .276 ($8/29$); Fritz, .267 ($4/15$); Grace, .277 ($13/47$); Isabel, .269 ($7/26$); Kathleen, .275 ($11/40$); Luther, .278 ($5/18$); Marjorie, .273 ($9/33$).

The Coin Collectors

Values: Dimes: $1.10, $2.80, $7.40, $9.10; Quarters: $8.50, $11.50, $17, $23.

Clue 1: Eileen isn't Edo, Nadia isn't Nim, Santos isn't Spar, and Trevor isn't Topp.

Clue 2: Edo isn't 11, Nim isn't 92 or 91, Spar isn't 68 or 74, Topp isn't 34 or 28; Eileen isn't 11, Nadia isn't 91 or 92, Santos isn't 74 or 68, Trevor isn't 28 or 34; and 28 isn't 34, 74 isn't 68, and 91 isn't 92.

Clue 3: Nadia does not have 34 quarters. $91 - 17 = 74$ and $28 - 17 = 11$, so Nadia has either 74 or 11 dimes. 34 is either with 91 or 28. It cannot be with 28, because they both start with T, so 34 is with 91, and Nadia has 74 dimes. You can then note that Nadia does not have the last name of Spar (74 starts with S). She also does not have 68 quarters. Nadia has 46 quarters (only one).

Clue 4: Nadia has 46 quarters: $46 \times 2 = 92$, so 28 goes with 92. Also, whoever has 28 dimes and 92 quarters is a boy, so Eileen cannot have 28 dimes, leaving Santos with 28 dimes and 92 quarters. Eileen has 91 dimes and 34 quarters and Trevor has 11 dimes and 68 quarters (only ones).

Clue 5: $28 - 11 = 17$. So, the Nim child has 11 dimes and the Edo child has 28 dimes. Therefore, Trevor's last name is Nim and Santos' last name is Edo.

Further Reasoning: Because of Clue 2, we know that Eileen's last name is not Topp (she has 34 quarters). Her last name is Spar (only one) and Nadia's last name is Topp (only one). Note that some students may be able to finish solving the puzzle using reasoning after Clue 4, whereas others will need clue 5.

Answers: Eileen Spar, 91 dimes ($9.10) and 34 quarters ($8.50) = $17.60; Nadia Topp, 74 dimes ($7.40) and 46 quarters ($11.50) = $18.90; Santos Edo, 28 dimes ($2.80) and 92 quarters ($23) = $25.80; Trevor Nim, 11 dimes ($1.10) and 68 quarters ($17) = $18.10.

Shop 'Til You Stop

Clue 1: Baseball card is 5:30.

Clue 2: Chuck is 9:00, so he can't be baseball cards [1], and he isn't soda, so soda isn't 9:00.

Clue 3: Candy bar is 1:15, candy bar is not Chuck [2].

Clue 4: Paulette isn't baseball cards, so she isn't 5:30 [1].

Clue 5: Lymon is crayons. He is 1:15 or 4:00 (2 ¾ hours after another time), so crayons is 1:15 or 4:00, but candy bar is 1:15 [3] so 4:00 must be crayons and Lymon.

Further Reasoning: Soda is 10:30 and dog food is 9:00 (only ones); Chuck is dog food [2]. Hixon is 2¾ hours before Lymon and crayons, so he is 1:15, which is candy bar [3]. Donnita is baseball cards, which is also 5:30 (only one) and Paulette is soda and 10:30.

Answers: Chuck, dog food, 9 a.m.; Donnita, baseball cards, 5:30 p.m.; Hixon, candy bar, 1:15 p.m.; Lymon, crayons, 4 p.m.; Paulette, soda, 10:30 a.m.

Summer Sitters

Chart: Monday: 5h 15m, 5h 45m, 6h 15m; Thursday: 4h 30m, 5h 45m, 6h 30m; Saturday: 5h 45m, 6h 15m, 7h.

Clue 1: Kamea sat from 2:15–8:45 p.m. on Thursday.

Clue 2: 1:00–6:15 p.m. on Monday is with 5h 45m (3:30–9:15 p.m.) on Saturday.

Clue 3: Tatum is 6h 15m on Monday (1:45–8:00 p.m.); she is not 5h 45m (3:30–9:15 p.m.) on Saturday. 1:45–8:00 p.m. on Monday does not go with 2:15–8:45 p.m. on Thursday (Kamea's time).

Clue 4: 1:45–8:00 p.m. goes with 3:45–9:30 p.m., Tatum is with 3:45–9:30 p.m. Lari sat from 5 to 9:30 p.m. on Thursday (only one).

Clue 5: 3:30–9:15 p.m. (5h 45m) on Saturday is also 4h 30m (5:00-9:30 p.m.) on Thursday, and that is Lari [4]. 3:30–9:15 p.m. on Saturday goes with 1:00–6:15 p.m. on Monday, so Lari sat Monday from 1:00–6:15 p.m. Kamea sat from 4:30–10:15 p.m. on Monday (only one).

Clue 6: Add Tatum and Kamea's Monday and Thursday times: Kamea sat for 12h 15m Monday and Thursday, whereas Tatum sat for 12h those days. Try Tatum with the remaining hours to see which time she would have to sit to have more hours than Kamea. If Tatum sat from 1:15–7:30 p.m. Saturday, she would only have 18h 15m total, whereas Kamea would have 19h 15m if she sat from 2:45–9:45 p.m. So, Tatum must have sat from 2:45–9:45 p.m. (19 total hours), and Kamea must have sat from 1:15–7:30 p.m. (18 hours and 30 minutes total) if Tatum made more money than Kamea.

Answers: Kamea, 5h 45m Monday, 6h 30m Thursday, 6h 15m Saturday = 18h 30m (18.5) × $3.50 = $64.75; Lari, 5h 15m Monday, 4h 30m Thursday, 5h 45m Saturday = 15h 30m (15.5) × $3.50 = $54.25; Tatum, 6h 15m Monday, 5h 45m Thursday, 7h Saturday = 19 h × $3.50 = $66.50 (Tatum made the most money).

Arduous Arithmetic

Correct computations: 6 km, 8 km, 11 km, 13 km; 3 kg, 8 kg, 10 kg, 14 kg.

Clue 1: Blaire isn't 5 mi or 22.046 pounds.

Clue 2: 6 ⅞ isn't Sabah or 10 kg; 10 kg isn't Ashley.

Clue 3: 8 ⅛ isn't 22.046, 8 km, or Maya; 22.046 isn't 8 km or Maya; 8 km isn't Maya. Then 22.046 (10 kg) is Sabah and 6 km (3 ¾ mi; only ones) and Sabah is 6 km. Maya is 6 ⅞ mi (10.75 km; only one). Blaire is 13 km (8 ⅛ mi) and Ashley is 8 km (5 mi; only ones).

Clue 4: 5 miles (8 km; Ashley [3]) is with 30.8644.

Clue 5: 3.75 kg (6.6138 pounds) is Maya (and 10.75 km); 8 kg (17.6368 pounds) is Blaire (and 12 km).

Answers: Ashley, 8 km (5 mi; answer was correct), 13 kg (30.8644 pounds; incorrect); Blaire, 12 km (8 ⅛ mi; incorrect), 8 kg (17.6368 pounds; correct); Maya, 10.75 km (6 ⅞ mi; incorrect), 3.75 kg (6.6138 pounds; incorrect); Sabah, 6 km (3 ¾ mi; correct), 10 kg (22.046 pounds; correct). Sabah was the "Math Marvel" for last week.

Winter in Wyoming

Clue 1: Ruby isn't -9, -7, or -2; L'Wella isn't -7, -1, or 10.

Clue 2: Dori isn't -9, -7, or -2; Aidan isn't -7, -1, or 10. .

Clue 3: Dori and Forbes aren't -9, -7, or -5 because at least three are colder; Trista isn't -9 or -7 because at least two are colder and she isn't 6 or 10 because at least two are warmer; Bentley and Hope aren't 2, 6, or 10 because at least three are warmer. If Dori isn't -5, Aidan is not -9 [2].

Clue 4: Forbes isn't -9, -7, -5, -2, or 2; Ruby isn't -9, -7, -2, -1, or 10.

Clue 5: L'Wella isn't -9, -5, or -2 (three are colder); Dori isn't 10 or 6 (two people are warmer); Aidan isn't -9, 2, or 6 (one is colder and three are warmer); Hope isn't -1 (four people are warmer) or -2 because Aidan's highest possible temperature is -2, and Hope's must be lower than that. Forbes is 10 (only one).

Clue 6: Aidan is -5 or -2, so Bentley would be -9 or -6, but there isn't -6, so Bentley must be -9 and Aidan is -5. So, Hope is -7 (only one).

Further Reasoning: From Clue 1, Ruby is 6 or 2; not 10 [4], not -1 [4], or -5 [Aidan], so L'Wella would be 2 or -2, but she isn't -2 (at least four are colder: Bentley, Hope, Aidan, and Dori), so she is 2 and Ruby is 6. From Clue 2, Dori isn't 10 [Forbes], 6 [Ruby], 2 [L'Wella], or -5 [Aidan], so she is -1 (only one) and 4 degrees warmer than Aidan. Trista is -2 (only one).

Answers: Aidan -5°; Bentley, -9°; Dori, -1°; Forbes, 10°, Hope -7°; L'Wella, 2°; Ruby, 6°; Trista, -2°.

Triathlon Times

Clue 1: 18m 27s run isn't with 29m 29s bike; 18m 27s run isn't with 6m 04s swim; and 29m 29s bike isn't with 6m 04s swim.

Clue 2: Elery biked for 23m 44s and swam for 5m 56s, so 23m 44s bike goes with 5m 56s swim.

Clue 3: Perry swam for 6m 04s; Alana ran for 18m 12s; 18m 12s run isn't with 6m 04s swim or 5m 56s swim; 23m 44s bike isn't with 18m 12s run.

Clue 4: 26m 15s bike is with 18m 12s run which is Alana, but isn't 6m 04s swim. Then 6m 04s swim [Perry, 3] is with 21m 09s bike (only one); 21m 09s bike (and Perry) isn't with 18m 27s run since 6m 04s swim isn't with 18m 27s run. Kalista biked for 29m 29s (only one); neither are with 18m 27 run. Then Elery is 18m 27s run (only one), which goes with 5m 56s swim and 23m 44s bike. And 26m 15s run isn't with 5m 17s swim (fastest), so it's 5m 59s swim (only one); 29m 29s bike is with 5m 17s swim, which isn't with 18m 12s run. Then 18m 12s run is with 5m 59s swim (only one), and those both go with Alana [3]; Kalista swam for 5m 17s (only one).

Clue 5: Kalista swam for 5m 17s [4], so three times that is 15m 51s. Add 2 minutes, and you find that she ran for 17m 51s; and Perry ran for 20m 13s.

Answers: Alana, 26m 15s bike, 18m 12s run, 5m 59s swim; Elery, 23m 44s bike, 18m 27s run, 5m 56s swim; Kalista, 29m 29s bike, 17m 51s run, 5m 17s swim; Perry, 21m 09s bike, 20m 13s run, 6m 04s swim.

Exponent² Components³

Missing numbers: 27, 64, 125, 216, and 343.

Clue 1: Rusty isn't (4³) 64. Rusty or 64 is Tuesday, but you can't mark it yet.

Clue 2: Elena is 216; Elena is not Wednesday; 216 is not Wednesday.

Clue 3: Cheri isn't Friday or 343, and 343 (7³) isn't Monday.

Clue 4: Cheri and Janna (girls) are not 64; Elena isn't 64 [2]; Rusty isn't 64 [1], so 64 is Mannix. Either Mannix or Rusty is Tuesday [1], so no girls are Tuesday. If Cheri isn't Tuesday, then 343 isn't Wednesday [3].

Clue 5: Rusty isn't Monday; Mannix isn't Friday.

Clue 6: Janna is not 125. 125 (5³) isn't the day before Janna, but could be two or more days before Janna, or some days after Janna. You can't mark anything yet, but will refer back to this clue. 4' 6" is with 109 lbs. [1], so Rishab is 109 lbs.

Clue 7: Mannix isn't Friday [5], so 7³ (343) must be Friday; Friday isn't Elena [216]. If 343 is Friday, then Cheri is Thursday [3, day before]. Cheri isn't 4³ or 6³, so Thursday isn't 4³ or 6³. Elena is Monday (only one); 216 is Monday [2]. 4'11

Further Reasoning: Mannix isn't Monday so Rusty isn't Tuesday [6, day after Mannix], but one of them is Tuesday [1], so Mannix must be Tuesday [Tuesday is 64, Clue 3] and Rusty must be Wednesday [7, day after Mannix]. So, Janna is Friday (only one); Friday is 7³, so Janna is 7³.

Janna is Friday, so 125 (5³) can't be Thursday [5, day before Janna], so 3³ is Thursday (only one) [and Cheri]. Then Rusty is 125 (only one) and 125 is Wednesday.

Answers: Cheri, 3³ (27), Thursday; Elena, 6³ (216), Monday; Janna, 7³ (343), Friday; Mannix, 4³ (64), Tuesday; Rusty, 5³ (125), Wednesday.

What Goes Around Comes Around

Correct answers for empty spaces: 2,700; 4,900; 10,400; 13,700; 69,000; 96,100; 587,900; 716,300.

Clue 1: Nelson isn't 2,653 or 4,892, Elizabeth isn't 2,653 or 716,294, and Steve isn't 587,932 or 716,294.

Clue 2: Rush isn't 2,653; 4,892; 587,932; or 716,294 and Elizabeth isn't 2,653; 4,892; 587,932; or 716,294. Faye isn't 10,393; 13,651; 68,978; or 96,102 and Yvette isn't 10,393; 13,651; 68,978, or 96,102.

Clue 3: Clarice isn't 2,653 or 4,892, Kent isn't 2,653 or 716,294, and Faye isn't 587,932 or 716,294. Nelson isn't 2,653 or 4,892 [1], Yvette isn't 2,653 or 716,294, and Rush isn't 587,932; or 716,294 [2].

Clue 4: Kent isn't 4,892 (4-digit); 716,294 [3], 587,932 (6-digit), or 10,393 (smallest 5-digit) and Elizabeth isn't 96,102 (largest 5-digit). Rush isn't 10,393 (smallest 5-digit) and Clarice isn't 587,932 or 716,294 (6-digit) or 96,102 (largest 5-digit). Then Nelson is 716,294 (has to be larger than Yvette). Yvette is 587,932 (only one).

Clue 5: After several trials, you should find that 2,653 × 26 = 68,978, so Faye is 2,653. Then Steve is 4,892 (only one).

Further Reasoning: In Clue 3, Clarice's number is larger than Kent's. The smallest possible number for Kent is 13,651, so Clarice's must be larger than that. Her only possibility is 68,978 and Kent is 13,651. Rush is 96,102 and Elizabeth is 10,393 (only ones).

Answers: Clarice, 68,978; Elizabeth, 10,393; Faye, 2,653; Kent, 13,651; Nelson, 716,294; Rush, 96,102; Steve, 4,892; Yvette, 587,932.

Students who correctly rounded to hundreds were: Elizabeth, Kent, and Yvette. Faye rounded ones incorrectly; Steve rounded hundreds incorrectly; Clarice and Rush rounded thousands incorrectly; Nelson rounded ones correctly.

Let's Hit the Slopes

Clue 1: Kipley could have spent $56 (if Tamiko's boots were $112), $74 (if Tamiko spent $148 on the jacket), $84 (if Tamiko spent $168 on her jacket), and $112 (if Tamiko spent $224 on the jacket). Eliminate $135 for Kipley and save the other information for later.

Clue 2: $74 boots isn't $148 jacket and $84 boots isn't $168 jacket.

Clue 3: The only possibility is $56 × 3 = $168 ($74 × 3 = $222 and the others are too large), so $56 boots is with $168 jacket.

Clue 4: Subtract $51 from the jacket prices: $186 − $51 = $135 (a boot price) and $125 − $51 = $74 (a boot price). Prita could be $135 or $74 on boots. Darlis could have spent $186 or $125 on a jacket. The same combinations go for Darlis' boots and Tamiko's jacket. Looking at the extra info for Clue 1, Tamiko needed to spend $112, $148, $168, or $224. We've just eliminated the last three, so Tamiko spent $112 on boots and Kipley spent $56 on boots. Max spent $84 on boots (only one).

Clue 5: The only possibility is for Kipley to have spent $168 on the jacket ($168 + $56 = $224). This means Prita spent $224 on the jacket. Max spent $148 on a jacket (only one).

Clue 6: We know Tamiko spent $112 on her boots, but only could have spent $125 or $186 on the jacket. There were no $13 boots, so Tamiko spent $186 on her jacket. That means Prita spent $74 on her boots. Darlis spent $135 on boots and $125 on a jacket (only ones).

Answers: Darlis, $135 boots, $125 jacket; Kipley, $56 boots, $168 jacket; Max, $84 boots, $148 jacket; Prita, $74 boots, $224 jacket; Tamiko, $112 boots, $186 jacket. Totals: Darlis = $260, Kipley = $224 (least), Max = $232, Prita = $296, Tamiko = $298 (most).

My Space

Chart for bedroom size: 132 sq. ft., 154 sq. ft., 156 sq. ft., 195 sq. ft.

Chart for weekly allowance: $143, $182, $234, $273.

Clue 1: 12-year-old isn't 11 × 12 (132 sq. ft.) or 12 × 13 (156 sq. ft.).

Clue 2: 10-year-old isn't Nate; 10-year-old isn't 11 × 12 (132 sq. ft.); Nate isn't 11 × 12 (132 sq. ft.).

Clue 3: 11 × 14 (154 sq. ft.) isn't $2.75 ($143) or $3.50 ($182); 11-year-old isn't $3.50.

Clue 4: 13 × 15 (195 sq. ft.) is not Lydia; 13 × 15 (195 sq. ft.) is not Nate.

Clue 5: 12-year-old isn't 13 × 15 (195 sq. ft.), so 12-year-old is 11 × 14 sq. ft. (only one); 12-year-old isn't $4.50 ($134), so 11 × 14 sq. ft. isn't $4.50; then it's $5.25 (only one). Then 12-year-old is $5.25 ($273).

Clue 6: 12 × 13 (156 sq. ft.) isn't $2.75, 11-year-old, or Dwight; $2.75 isn't 11-year-old or Dwight; 11-year-old isn't Dwight. Then 11-year-old is $4.50 (only one), but not 12 × 13, so $4.50 is not 12 × 13. Then 12 × 13 is $3.50 (only one), but not Dwight, so Dwight isn't $3.50. And 11-year-old is not Dwight, so Dwight is not $4.50 ($234), he's $5.25 (only one), which is also the 12-year-old and 11 × 14.

Further Reasoning: Then 13 × 15 is Twyla (only one), Nate is 12 × 13 [also $3.50 because 12 × 13 is $3.50] and Lydia is 11 × 12 (only ones). Both 12 × 13 and $3.50 are either the 10-year-old or 13-year-old, but Nate isn't the 10-year-old, so 12 × 13, $3.50, and Nate all go with 13 years old. So, the 10-year-old is 13 × 15 (195 sq. ft.), Twyla, and $2.75 (only ones); 11-year-old is 11 × 12 (132 sq. ft.), Lydia, and $4.50.

Answers: Dwight, 12 years, 154 sq. ft., $5.25; Lydia, 11 years, 132 sq. ft., $4.50; Nate, 13 years, 156 sq. ft., $3.50; Twyla, 10 years, 195 sq. ft., $2.75.

Land of 10,000 Lakes

Clue 1: Rochester goes with Albert Lea; Gilman isn't Rochester or Albert Lea.

Clue 2: Moorhead goes with Brainerd; Clausen isn't Moorhead or Brainerd.

Clue 3: Medford is Red Wing; Medford isn't Hibbing or Willmar; Red Wing isn't Hibbing or Willmar. Medford isn't Brainerd, so it isn't Moorhead [2] either.

Clue 4: Clausen goes with Hutchinson; then Hutchinson isn't Moorhead, Brainerd, or Red Wing; Hutchinson isn't Albert Lea so Clausen isn't Albert Lea. Gilman goes with Duluth; Duluth doesn't go with Red Wing (not Gilmans). Gilman isn't Brainerd, so it isn't Moorhead [2] either.

Clue 5: The three "M" cities are Mankato, Marshall, and Montevideo. It isn't Moorhead because Moorhead goes with Brainerd (does not start with M). Hennepin isn't with Mankato, Marshall, and Montevideo; and Medford isn't with Mankato, Marshall, and Montevideo [3]. Then Faribaults went to Mankato (only one), so they also went to Marshall and Montevideo. Hennepins drove to Brainerd (only one) and to Moorhead [2]. Then Medfords went to Albert Lea (only one) and Rochester [1] which both go with Red Wing [3]. Hennepins went to St. Cloud (only one), which goes with Brainerd and Moorhead [2].

Clue 6: Willmar goes with Fergus Falls. Then Hibbing is with International Falls (only one). Gilmans didn't go to Fergus Falls, so they went to International Falls (only one) and Clausens went to Fergus Falls (and Willmar); then Gilmans went to Hibbing (only one), which goes with International Falls.

Answers: Clausen, Hutchinson, Willmar, Fergus Falls; Faribault, Mankato, Marshall, Montevideo; Gilman, Duluth, Hibbing, International Falls; Hennepin, St. Cloud, Moorhead, Brainerd; Medford, Rochester, Albert Lea, Red Wing.

Speed Doesn't Pay, You Do!

Mph over/fine section: 12 mph × $8 = $96; 15 mph × $6 = $90; 16 mph × $5 = $80; 18 mph × $7 = $126. NOTE: You may find that $5 × 18 mph = $90 and $6 × 15 mph = $90; also $6 × 16 mph = $96 and $8 × 12 mph = $96. But $8 × 15 = $120, $8 × 16 = $128, and $8 × 18 = $144, which are not choices, so $8 × 12 = $96 must be correct; then $96 can't be $6 × 16 which leaves $6 × 15 = $90. Then $5 × 18 = $90 is not correct.

Clue 1: Justin isn't 11:37 p.m. and Melissa isn't 2:13 a.m.

Clue 2: Malls open in the morning around 9:00–10:00 a.m., so assume 9:21 a.m. is for the one opening *her* store (which isn't a boy), so 9:21 a.m. isn't Justin or Travis; 9:21 a.m. girl isn't 12 mph over; Travis isn't $80 so isn't 16 mph (16 × 5 = $80), or 18 mph, so isn't $126 (18 × $7 = $126).

Clue 3: Justin isn't $5 for each mph over, so isn't $80 or 16 mph ($5 × 16 = $80); Larissa isn't $8 for each mph over, so isn't $96 or 12 mph ($8 × 12 = $96); Larissa isn't $80 (so isn't 16 mph), then Melissa is $80 and 16 mph (only ones); and Justin isn't $126 (so isn't 18 mph), then Larissa is 18 mph and $126 (only ones). Larissa paid $7 per mile over, and Justin's was

87

costlier, so he paid $8 per mile over (12 mph × $8 = $96). Then Travis was 15 mph over and $90.

Clue 4: One would leave elementary school at about 4 in the afternoon, so assume 4:29 p.m. doesn't go with $126; then Larissa, $126, and 18 mph don't go with 4:29 p.m.

Clue 5: $96 [Justin] isn't 2:13 a.m. because one got a ticket earlier than that, so he is 4:29 p.m. (the teacher); then 16 mph isn't 9:21 a.m. (the shop owner) who is either 15 or 18 mph. She was driving faster than Travis [2] who is 15 mph over, so 9:21 a.m. is 18 mph; that is Larissa and $126. Travis is 2:13 a.m. (15 mph and $90) and Melissa is 11:37 p.m. (16 mph and $80; only ones).

Answers: Justin, 4:29 p.m., 12 mph, $96; Larissa, 9:21 a.m., 18 mph, $126; Melissa, 11:37 p.m., 16 mph, $80; Travis, 2:13 a.m., 15 mph, $90.

Let's Hit the Road, Girls

Clue 1: Heidi is not $81.27 (most gas); Kat is not $55.29 (least gas). Kat is not $74.29 (most motel) or $442.32 (most shopping); Heidi is not $59.68 (least motel) or $368.64 (least shopping).

Clue 2: Kat spent less than Heidi [1] and Meredith on motel, so she isn't $74.29 or $69.42. There is a difference of $4.87, so Meredith can't be $74.29 (Kat isn't $69.42) and she isn't $59.68 (least). Meredith is not $55.29 (least gas) and Kat is not $81.27 (most gas). Heidi isn't $72.61 for gas (Kat isn't $81.27 [2], and Meredith spent more than Heidi).

Clue 3: Motel of $59.68 × 7 = $417.76 is the only combination that works, so $59.68 motel goes with $417.76 shopping; neither are Heidi [1] or Meredith [2].

Clue 4: The only difference that works is $69.42 − $5.47 = $63.95, so they go together.

Clue 5: ⅛ = .125. Multiply each shopping total by .125; only combination that fits is $442.32 × .125 = $55.29; Maggie is $55.29 gas and Heidi is $442.32 shopping; $55.29 gas isn't with $442.32 shopping. $55.29 gas is not $69.42 motel, so Maggie is not $69.42 motel. Heidi is $63.95 gas (only one) then Kat is $72.61 and Meredith is $81.27 gas (only ones). $63.95 gas is $69.42 motel, so Heidi is $69.42 motel [$442.32 shopping]. Maggie is $74.29 motel (only one); then $59.68 is Kat and $64.55 is Meredith (only ones). Kat is $59.68 motel, which is $417.76 shopping, so Kat is $417.76 shopping.

Clue 6: Subtract $318.91 from $368.64 and $393.20 (yet unmatched combinations); the difference that works is $393.20 shopping − $318.91 = $74.29 motel, so they go together. Then $368.64 shopping is with $64.55 motel (only one) and Meredith. Maggie is $393.20 shopping (only one).

Answers: Heidi, $63.95 gas, $69.42 motel, $442.32 shopping; Kat, $72.61 gas, $59.68 motel, $417.76 shopping; Maggie, $55.29 gas, $74.29 motel, $393.20 shopping; Meredith, $81.27 gas, $64.55 motel, $368.64 shopping.

Sweet Treat

There are two candies that weighed 3 lbs total. When marking, consider just one, not both.

Chart: Caramels, Jenntrie, 4 lbs, 75 cents per lb, $3; cashew clusters, Carnine, 3 lbs, $5 per lb, $15; choc. cherries, Ramsey,

1 ½ lbs, $3.50 per lb, $5.25; fudge, Naomi, 2 ½ lbs, $3 per lb, $7.50; peanut brittle, Emma, 3 lbs, $3.50 per lb, $10.50.

Clue 1: Write $5 price per lb under cashew clusters.

Clue 2: Ramsey is chocolate cherries. He can't be $3 (no $6), $10.50 (no $21), or $15 (no $30). Emma is $10.50 or $15 (double Ramsey's) so isn't $3.00, $5.25 or $7.50.

Clue 3: Fudge is 2½ × $3 = $7.50, which can't be Ramsey [choc. cherries, 2], so Ramsey is $5.25 and Emma is $10.50 [2]. To find Ramsey's price per pound, divide $5.25 by different pounds: $5.25 ÷ 4 = $1.3125 per lb (not likely), $5.25 ÷ 3 = $1.75 per lb, $5.25 ÷ 2 ½ = $2.10 per lb (?, maybe), or $5.25 ÷ 1 ½ = $3.50 per lb (all could be). Caramel is 75% less than $3.00; 75% of $3.00 is $.75 per pound. Caramels can't be Emma because $.75 × the greatest weight (4 lbs) is only $3, and Emma is $10.50.

Clue 4: 100% more means 1 + 100%, or double. The only combination that works is 1½ × 100% more (or 1 ½ × 2) = 3 lbs., so choc. cherries [Ramsey, 2] sold 1 ½ lbs. His price per lb is $5.25 ÷ 1 ½ = $3.50 per lb and $5.25 is 1 ½ lbs. A girl sold 3 lbs of brittle, so one of the 3 lbs is not Carnine [boy, Intro.], but he could be the other 3 lbs. (Be careful when eliminating!)

Clue 5: Ramsey sold 1 ½ lbs [4], so cashew clusters is 3 lbs (twice as much as Ramsey); he's a boy, so cashew clusters (3 lbs) is Carnine. Cashew clusters were $5 per lb [1], so Carnine and his 3 lbs are $15 ($5 per pound).

Clue 6: Jenntrie is .20 (20%) × $15 = $3 for her candy; so Naomi is $7.50 (only one), which is fudge [3] and 2 ½ lbs. ($7.50).

Further Reasoning: Emma isn't caramels [3], so caramels are with Jenntrie whose price per pound is $.75 [3]; .75 × 3 lbs = $2.25 (not a choice), so .75 × 4 lbs = $3.00 price. Then Emma is peanut brittle, $10.50, and 3 lbs; $10.50 ÷ 3 lbs = $3.50 per pound.

Answers: Jenntrie, 4 lbs, $3; Carnine, 3 lbs, $15; Ramsey, 1 ½ lbs, $5.25; Naomi, 2 ½ lbs, $7.50; Emma, 3 lbs, $10.50.

Flower Power

Amounts: $1,048; $1,261; $1,407; $1,596; $1,755; $3,300; $3,528; $4,900; $5,491; $6,420; $6,592.

Clue 1: Dahlia isn't March 2, May 27, February 28, March 17, or May 6. Jasmine and Violet are not June 21, June 19, May 27, January 15, February 28, May 6, or January 8. Dahlia, Violet, and Jasmine are not $1,048; $1,261; $1,407; $1,596; $1,755; $3,300; $3,258; or $4,900.

Clue 2: May 24 ($1,048) is not Camellia, Dahlia, Ginger, Heather, Iris, Jasmine, Lily, Zinnia, or Violet [1].

Clue 3: Lily, Rosa, Iris, and Amaryllis are not $4,900; $5,491; $6,126; $6,420; or $6,592.

Clue 4: April 4 ($4,900) is not Laurel or Ginger.

Clue 5: Heather, Jasmine, Lily and Zinnia are not $1,048 [known]; $1,261; $1,407; $1,596; $1,755; $6,126; $6,420; or $6,592. Jasmine is $5,491 (only one). Then Violet is $6,420 (only one). Dahlia is $6,592 (only one).

Clue 6: $3,300 × 2 = $6,600. Subtract 8 so $6,600 − 8 = $6,592 [Dahlia]; then Heather is $3,300. Lily is $3,528 and Zinnia is $4,900 (only ones).

Clue 7: $3,300 (Heather) − $108 = $3,192; $3,192 ÷ 2 = $1,596, so Rosa's mom gave $1,596.

Clue 8: Camellia was born on June 21 (2 weeks after June 7).

Clue 9: Ginger was born on May 27 (9 days before June 5).

Further Reasoning: Laurel is $6,126 (May 6; only one). Iris is $1,261 (April 13; only one) and Amaryllis is $1,048 (March 2; only one).

Answers: Amaryllis, $1,048, 5-24, March 2; Camellia, $1,407, 6-7, June 21; Dahlia, $6,592, 8-24, January 8; Ginger, $1,755, 6-5, May 27; Heather, $3,300, 2-20, January 15; Iris, $1,261, 9-7, April 13; Jasmine, $5,491, 3-23, March 17; Laurel, $6,126, 10-21, May 6; Lily, $3,528, 12-6, February 28; Rosa, $1,596, 8-4, June 19; Violet, $6,420, 2-14, April 30; Zinnia, $4,900, 12-25, April 4. The total raised was $43,424.

Out to Lunch: Part I

Each can spend $5.28 ($26.40 ÷ 5 = $5.28).

Missing amounts: ⅝ = $3.30; ⅔ = $3.52; ¾ = $3.96; ⅚ = $4.40. Change: $1.98, $1.76, $1.32, and $.88. Dad spent $5.28 [intro.].

Clue 1: This states what mozz. is.

Clue 2: Barry had the burger and fries. He didn't have $.88, which is ⅙ of $5.28, so he didn't spend ⅚ ($4.40) and burger/fries isn't ⅚ ($4.40).

Clue 3: Carrie didn't have salad and milk; Carrie didn't spend ⅚ ($4.40); salad and milk didn't cost ⅚ ($4.40).

Clue 4: $1.32 is ¼ of $5.28, so one of the fruits cost $3.96 (¾). It isn't Barry [2], so burger/fries and salad/milk aren't $3.96. A girl bought one fruit (clue says *she*), but you don't know who bought the other fruit.

Clue 5: A boy had salad and milk, so not Carrie [3] or Merrie [girls, Intro.]; it's Gary because the other boy had a burger and fries. Salad/milk isn't ¾ [fruit, 4] or ⅚ [3] so Gary isn't ¾ or ⅚. Then ⅚ ($4.40) is Merrie (only one), so Carrie is ¾ ($3.96; only one). Salad isn't $1.76 change (⅓), so salad didn't cost ⅔ ($3.52) and Gary didn't pay $3.52; he paid $3.30 (⅝; only one). Barry paid $3.52 (⅔) for his burger/fries (only one).

Clue 6: Vegetarians don't eat meat, so Carrie didn't have meat (burger or chicken); she ate cheese sticks [1] and fruit (only one). Then Merrie had chicken and fruit (only one) which cost $4.40 (⅚). Carrie's cheese and fruit cost $3.96 (¾; only one).

Answers: Barry, burger and fries, $3.52 (⅔); Carrie, mozzarella cheese sticks and fruit, $3.96 (¾); Gary, salad and milk, $3.30 (⅝); Merrie, chicken and fruit, $4.40 (⅚).

Out to Lunch: Part II

From Out to Lunch: Part I, you can fill in the missing amounts: ⅙ = $.88; ¼ = $1.32; ⅓ = $1.76; ⅜ = $1.98.

Clue 1: Gary ate salad [Part I] and found his money [⅜ = $1.98] on the garage floor. He didn't need pencils or cards. Make note, but there is not a place to mark it on the matrix.

Clue 2: Merrie is car or coat pocket, not bedroom or garage [1], and she didn't want a milkshake. Make note, but there is not a place to mark it on the matrix.

Clue 3: Adrienne is cards, so isn't Gary's friend [1] because he didn't want cards; she isn't garage floor or $1.98 (⅜) [1].

Clue 4: The clue says *boys*, so one pair of friends is two boys, car, and pencils. It isn't Gary because his money was found in the garage, Adrienne or Necia because they are girls, so it must

be Barry and $1.76 (⅔) [Part I]; then Adrienne and Necia are not $1.76 (⅔) or car. The amount in the coat pocket was $.88 (only one) and $1.32 was found in the bedroom (only one).

Clue 5: Merrie is ⅙ and $.88 [Part I], so she is friends with Momed and needed hair clips; $.88 (⅙) is Momed, but he is not car or garage, he's coat pocket [4]. Jamason is car (only one) and must be Barry's friend; so he is $1.76 (⅓) and pencils. Adrienne is $1.32 (¼) and Necia is $1.98 (only ones).

Further Reasoning: Adrienne is bedroom and Necia is garage (only ones). Necia is Gary's friend, so she's not cards [1]. She's milkshake and Adrienne is cards.

Answers: Adrienne, bedroom dresser, $1.32 (¼; Carrie, deck of cards); Jamason, car, $1.76 (⅓; Barry, pencils); Momed, coat pocket, $.88 (⅙; Merrie, hair clips); Necia, garage floor, $1.98 (⅜; Gary, milkshake).

You Can Bank on This

Clue 1: $175 is not Lincoln Savings or West Trust.

Clue 2: Yamini isn't Bank of U.S., 5% or 7%; Bank of U.S. isn't 6.5% or 7%.

Clue 3: West Trust isn't $100 or $125 and isn't $175 [1], so it is $250. Then 6.5% is $175 [not Lincoln or West Trust, 1], so 6.5% is not Lincoln or West Trust; then it's State Bank (only one) and State Bank is $175.

Clue 4: Malati isn't $100 or State Bank; State Bank is $175 and 6.5%, so Malati is not $175 or 6.5%; Malati is $250 (more money than State Bank, which is $175) and West Trust [3].

Clue 5: Chandra isn't $100 (least), $125 (difference of only $25), or $250 [Malati, 4], so she is $175 (State Bank and 6.5%); then Yamini is 5.75% (only one) and 5.75% must be $75 less, so it's $100 and Yamini is $100 and Lincoln (only one). Lincoln is 5.75%. Therefore, Bank of U.S. is 5% (only one). Indira is Bank of U.S. (5%) and $125 (only ones); West Trust (Malati and $250) is 7% (only one).

Answers: Chandra, State Bank, 6.5%, $175; Indira, Bank of U.S., 5%, $125; Malati, West Trust, 7%, $250; Yamini, Lincoln Savings, 5.75%, $100. Totals: Chandra $186.38; Indira $131.25; Malati $267.50; Yamini $105.75.

Interest incomes: Chandra $11.38; Indira $6.25; Malati $17.50; Yamini $5.75. Malati has the largest deposit and interest rate, so she also has the largest interest income.

Vacation Vertigo

Clue 1: White is not 23rd or 2164; 2164 is not 3rd or Brown.

Clue 2: 259 × 8 = 2072, so 8th floor is room 2072, which is not Gray or Gold. So, Gold is not 8th and Gray isn't 8th (259 × 8) or 3rd (lower than 8th).

Clue 3: A family has a higher floor than the Grays, so they're not the 23rd floor. Some family has a room number higher than Green, so Green isn't room 2475. Gray isn't that family, so Gray is not 2475. The family with a higher room number than Greens is either 15th or 23rd.

Clue 4: 165 × 15 = 2475, so 15th floor is room 2475, which is not Gold or Brown and they are not 15th floor. Room 2475 is White (only one), so White is 15th floor, which leaves 9th floor for Gray (only one) and 23rd floor for the family with a higher room number than Greens, so 23rd isn't Green.

Clue 5: 255 × 9 = 2295, so 9th floor is room 2295 [Gray, 3]. Then 23rd floor is room 2164 (only one) for the family with a higher room number than Green, which must be 2072 on 8th floor.

Room 2164 isn't Brown [1], but it is 23rd so 23rd isn't Brown; it's Gold (only one) and Gold is room 2164. 3rd floor is room 2581 (only one). Then Browns are room 2381 on 3rd floor.

Answers: Gold, 23rd, 2164; Brown, 3rd, 2381; Gray, 9th, 2295; Green, 8th, 2072; White, 15th, 2475.

Put It in the Bank

Clue 1: Cameron is not the three larger totals; Bryant is not the three smaller totals.

Clue 2: Reed isn't $82.11 or $98.74; Judson isn't $82.11 or $205.36; Cameron isn't highest three [1].

Clue 3: Clarke and Baker are not Reed or the three lowest totals; combine clues 2 and 3 to find that Reed isn't $197.48, $205.36 (Clarke and Baker have more), $82.11, or $98.74 (Judson and Cameron have less); Judson is not the three highest or the lowest total; Cameron is lower than at least four people (Clarke, Baker, Reed, and Judson), so he isn't the four largest amounts. Reed, Judson, Cameron are not Clarke or Baker. Because Cameron is $82.11 or $98.74, Bryant is $164.22 or $197.48 [1]; he's not $205.36.

Clue 4: Reed and Bryant are not Mr. Morris. Morris had less than Reed, Clarke, and Baker [3], so isn't the three highest.

Clue 5: Judson is $102.68 or $98.74 [2], so Baker is $205.36 or $197.48. DeVry is $98.74 or $82.11 (less than Judson whose greatest possibility is $102.68).

Clue 6: Malloy isn't $205.36, then Lee is (only one); Malloy isn't $82.11, then Cameron is $82.11 (only one) and Bryant is $164.22 [1]. Reed is $102.68 (only one), Malloy is $197.48, and Judson is $98.74 (only ones). DeVry is less than half of Malloy ($197.48), so he is $82.11 and Cameron. Baker is not $164.22; Bryant is $164.22, so Bryant is not Baker. Reed is not Morris; Reed is $102.68, so $102.68 is not Morris; Morris is $98.74 (only one) and Judson.

Clue 7: Judson Morris is half of Baker [4], so he put in $98.74; Malloy Baker is $197.48.

Clue 8: Lee is not Ferris; Lee is $205.36, so Ferris is $102.68 and Reed. Lee is not Hastings, but Lee is $205.36, so Hastings is not $205.36; he is $164.22 (and Bryant). Clarke is $205.36 (only one), so he is Lee.

Answers: Bryant Hastings, $164.22; Cameron DeVry, $82.11; Judson Morris, $98.74; Lee Clarke, $205.36; Malloy Baker, $197.48; Reed Ferris, $102.68.

Bike-a-Thon

Chart of Miles × Pledges = Totals

~~9.45~~	~~11.20~~	13.65	15.40	17.15	19.00
~~11.48~~	13.60	16.58	18.70	20.83	23.80
12.83	15.20	18.53	20.90	23.28	26.60
13.50	16.00	19.50	22.00	24.50	28.00
14.31	16.96	20.67	23.32	25.97	~~29.68~~
15.31	18.14	22.11	24.95	27.78	~~31.75~~

Gray are correct combinations in clues.

From calculations, eliminate combinations 2.7 mi. × $3.50, 2.7 mi. × $4.25, 3.2 mi. × $3.50 (less than $12.83); 5.6 mi. × $5.30 and 5.6 mi. × $5.67 (more than $28.00). Circle $12.83 and $28.00 on chart—they are two combinations, so 2.7 mi is with $4.75 and 5.6 mi is with $5.00.

Clue 1: Benjie isn't $5.67 pledge (high), $5.00, or 5.6 mi. ($5.00 × 5.6 mi. = $28 total, which is the highest, so it can't be Benjie's); John isn't $3.50 pledge (low), $4.75 or 2.7 mi. ($4.75 × 2.7 = $12.83 total, which is the lowest, so it can't be John's).

Clue 2: Circle $16.96 because someone donated that total. On the chart, it is a combination (3.2 mi × $5.30). Camryn didn't ride 3.2, but she is .5 less, so she rode 2.7 mi. and is $4.75 for the total of $12.83. Mark 3.2 with $5.30. It's a girl, so either Fylecia or Lexie are 3.2 and $5.30.

Clue 3: John did not donate $28, so you can eliminate $5 and 5.6 mi for him. Fylecia did not donate $12.83 (she did not donate the least).

Clue 4: Fylecia was not 3.2, so Lexie is [2]. Lexie is $5.30, so Fylecia cannot be $5.67. John's pledge is higher than $5.30, so he must be $5.67. John and Fylecia both earned more than $16.96 (Lexie's total), but John's total donation was less than Fylecia's. Remember this for later.

Clue 5: Wallace's total was $20.83. The only option on the chart is for Wallace to have ridden 4.9 mi on a $4.25 pledge. Mark these in the grid. Fylecia earned $5 per mi and Benjie earned $3.50 per mi (only ones).

Clue 6: We know Wallace rode 4.9 mi. So, Fylecia must have ridden 5.6 mi. If Benjie rode further than John, he rode 4.4 mi and John rode 3.9 mi. To finish the chart, Benjie earned $15.40 and John earned $22.11.

Further Reasoning: Benjie is the higher miles, so he is 4.4 mi and John is 3.9 mi; then 4.4 mi is with $3.50 pledge (donation of $15.40) and 3.9 mi is with $5.67 pledge (donation of $22.11).

Answers: Benjie, 4.4 mi, $3.50 pledge, $15.40 total; Camryn, 2.7 mi, $4.75 pledge, $12.83 total; Fylecia, 5.6 mi, $5.00 pledge, $28.00 total; John, 3.9 mi, $5.67 pledge, $22.11 total; Lexie, 3.2 mi, $5.30 pledge, $16.96 total; Wallace, 4.9 mi, $4.25 pledge, $20.83 total.

Lightning Leap

Clue 1: Audi BHP isn't 300, Audi isn't 3,303 lbs, and 500 BHP isn't 3,303 lbs.

Clue 2: Corvette isn't 300, 415, or 420 BHP; BMW isn't 415, 420, or 500 BHP; 400 BHP must be Corvette or BMW, so no other cars have 400 BHP. The only weights with a difference of 76 are 3,290 lbs (must be Corvette) and 3,366 lbs (must be BMW); so 3,366 lbs isn't 415, 420, or 500; 3290 lbs isn't 300, 415, or 420.

Clue 3: Shelby isn't 300 BHP and Porsche isn't 500 BHP. (Depending on succeeding clues, if Porsche is 400 or 415, Shelby can't be 415 or 420, but they cannot be ruled out.)

Clue 4: The Porsche isn't 3,290 lbs [2, Corvette], 400 BHP isn't 3,908 lbs, and Porsche isn't 400 BHP; 400 BHP is either Corvette or BMW [2].

Clue 5: From Clue 2, Corvette weighed 3,290 and BMW was 76 lbs more, so BMW is 300 BHP. Corvette is 400 BHP [2]; 400

90

BHP is 3,290 lbs. That leaves 415 or 420 BHP for Porsche, so Shelby must be 500 BHP (at least 20 more) [3].

Clue 6: The 500 BHP car [5, Shelby] must weigh 3,908 lbs because adding 600 lbs to the lightest car (3,290 lbs) is 3,890 lbs or more; 500 BHP is 3,908 lbs (both Shelby).

Porsche is 3,308 lbs and Audi is 3,592 lbs (only ones); from Clue 1, Audi must have 420 BHP (more than 3,303 lb car, which is Porsche), and Porsche has 415 BHP.

Answers: Audi, 420 BHP, 3,592 lbs; BMW, 300 BHP, 3,366 lbs; Corvette, 400 BHP, 3,290 lbs; Ford Shelby, 500 BHP, 3,908 lbs; Porsche, 415 BHP, 3,303 lbs.

I Beg Your PARdon

Clue 1: Fran's bogies could be holes 3, 4, 5 or 7, 8, 9; Lawson's bogies could be holes 1, 2, 3, 4, 5, but not 7 or 8 (only two holes between his pars on 6 and 9).

Clue 2: No bogies on holes 2 or 6, so Lawson must be bogies on holes 3, 4, and 5 to be consecutive (score is 5, 5, 4).

Clue 3: Lawson got 7 on Hole 1 and Fran got 4 on Hole 1.

Clue 4: Ira and Rochelle got 4 on Hole 1 and Hole 6.

Clue 5: Wheeler, Ira, and Fran got 5 on Hole 5; Wheeler could have another double bogie on Hole 1, 7, or 9 and Fran could have another double bogie on Hole 3, 7, or 9.

Clue 6: Lawson's triple bogies must be on Holes 7 and 8 (only spaces available; scores of 6 and 7).

Clue 7: Ira made par on 2 and 4; 2 and 8; or 4 and 8; Wheeler made triple bogies on 2 and 6; 6 and 8; or 2 and 8.

Clue 8: Bogie on 3, 4, 9; 3, 4, 8; or 1, 7, and 8 isn't Lawson or Fran [3 consecutive, 1] so Fran must be triple bogie on Hole 4, which is a score of 7. Fran's bogies must be Holes 7, 8, 9 [1] to be consecutive (scores are 4, 5, 5). Bogie on 3, 4, 9 and 3, 4, 8 isn't Wheeler because he had par on Hole 4, so Wheeler is bogie on 1, 7, 8 (scores are 6, 4, 5). Bogies on 3, 4, 8 and 3, 4, 9 are Ira or Rochelle.

Clue 9: Fran is par on Hole 2 and birdie on 9, so it must be Rochelle who had double bogies on 2 and 9 (scores 5 and 6).

Further Reasoning: In Clue 2, Ira made par on 2 or 6, but he had a birdie on Hole 6 [4], so he got par on Hole 2 (score of 3). In Clue 5, Wheeler double bogied on 5 and another odd hole, which must be 9 because Hole 1 was bogie, Hole 4 was par, Hole 7 was bogie (score of 6). Fran double bogied on 5 and another odd hole which must be 3 because Hole 1 was birdie and Holes 7 and 9 were bogies (score of 6). In Clue 7, Wheeler made triple bogies on 2 and 6; 6 and 8; or 2 and 8. His Hole 8 was a bogie [8], so his triple bogies were 2 and 6 (scores of 6 and 8). Ira made one par on Hole 2 [2] and the other on Hole 8 (only one; score of 4). In Clue 8, Rochelle had a double bogie on Hole 9, so she can't be the one who had bogies on Holes 3, 4, 9 and she must be bogies on Holes 3, 4, 8 (scores of 5, 5, 5); then Ira must be bogies on 3, 4, 9 (scores of 5, 5, 5). Someone scored 49 [2]. Fran got 44, Ira got 41, Rochelle got 40, and Wheeler got 48, so Lawson got 49. His score on Holes 1, 3, 4, 5, 6, 7, 8, and 9 is 43, so Hole 2 must be 6 (triple bogie).

Answers: Fran: 4, 3, 6, 7, 5, 5, 4, 5, 5 = 44; Ira: 4, 3, 5, 5, 5, 4, 6, 4, 5 = 41; Lawson: 7, 6, 5, 5, 4, 5, 6, 7, 4 = 49; Rochelle: 4, 5, 5, 5, 3, 4, 3, 5, 6 = 40; Wheeler: 6, 6, 4, 4, 5, 8, 4, 5, 6 = 48; Rochelle won the game with the lowest score.

Jean "Green"

Clue 1: Lowe isn't Tuesday, 6.5% tax, or $36.99; Tuesday isn't 6.5% tax or $36.99; 6.5% is with $36.99.

Clue 2: Blake isn't Monday or Thursday.

Clue 3: Gage isn't Monday or Wednesday.

Clue 4: Thursday is not $36.99 (nor 6.5%), Roy, or 5.5%. Roy is not $36.99, 6.5%, or 5.5%. If two came before $36.99, $36.99 (and 6.5%) are Wednesday. Roy cannot be Wednesday.

Clue 5: Tuesday and Wednesday are not 6%, nor $37.69; $37.69 is not 6%.

Clue 6: $36.25 is 7% tax; 6% is $34.75, and 5.5% is $37.69 (only ones).

Further Reasoning: The $37.69 jeans were not bought Thursday (which is not 5.5%). They were bought on Monday. Roy did not buy the $37.69 jeans, so he did not shop Monday; he shopped Tuesday. Gage shopped Thursday, Lowe shopped Monday, and Blake shopped Wednesday (only ones). Blake is $36.99 and 6.5%. Lowe is $37.69 and 5.5%. 6% is Thursday and 7% is Tuesday (only ones), so Gage is 6% and Roy is 7%. Therefore, Roy spent $36.25 and Gage spent $34.75 (only ones).

Answers: Blake, Wed., 6.5% tax, $36.99; Gage, Thu., 6% tax, $34.75; Lowe, Mon., 5.5% tax, $37.69; Roy, Tue., 7% tax, $36.25.

Two Pieces of Pizza

Chart: first slice: .438, .462, .529, .533, .556; second slice: .444, .467, .471, .538, .563.

Clue 1: This clue seems irrelevant, but you will need the information later. Write bacon beside Horton and Ionia's names.

Clue 2: Bristow and Horton aren't $\frac{5}{9}$ (.556; largest 1st slice) or $\frac{4}{9}$ (.444; smallest 2nd slice).

Clue 3: First slice .438 ($\frac{7}{16}$) is pepperoni, so .563 ($\frac{9}{16}$) second slice must be pepperoni (its complement); second slice .444 ($\frac{4}{9}$) is sausage, so .556 ($\frac{5}{9}$) first slice must be sausage (its complement). Write pepperoni and sausage above the four sizes.

Clue 4: Ackley isn't .438, .529, or .556 (first) and Denver isn't .444, .471, or .563 (second) because they do not have differences of .005.

Clue 5: $\frac{7}{16}$ isn't with $\frac{9}{16}$, $\frac{6}{13}$ isn't with $\frac{7}{13}$, $\frac{9}{17}$ isn't with $\frac{8}{17}$, $\frac{8}{15}$ isn't with $\frac{7}{15}$, $\frac{5}{9}$ isn't with $\frac{4}{9}$. (You may have already marked this when you read the introduction.)

Clue 6: Bristow's first slice is either .462 or .533 of a pizza and Ionia's second slice is either .467 or .538 of a pizza (only combinations that work).

Further Reasoning: Ackley had the .444 sausage slice (only one). The $\frac{5}{9}$ slice doesn't go with .438 or .529 or .556. Ionia's first slice must be larger than her second slice, so she is not .438 or .462. If Ionia's second slice is cheese [6], then her first slice must be bacon [1]. Therefore, she is not .556 on the first slice. Denver ate the .556 sausage slice first, Horton had the .438 pepperoni slice first, and Ionia had the .529 slice (only ones). Ionia's .529 slice is a bacon slice. If Ionia's second slice is smaller than her first, she must have .467 as her second slice. Therefore, Bristow's first slice was .462 and taco [6]. Denver had a .538 second slice and Ackley had a .533 cheese slice first (only ones). Horton's second slice is bacon, so he didn't eat the

.563 pepperoni slice. He had the .471 bacon slice. Bristow had the .563 pepperoni slice.

Answers: Ackley, .533 (cheese), .444 (sausage); Bristow, .462 (taco), .563 (pepperoni); Denver, .556 (sausage), .538 (taco); Horton, .438 (pepperoni), .471 (bacon); Ionia, .529 (bacon), .467 (cheese).

Algeboy Class

Correct answers in solving for n: P1: n = 6, P2: n = 4, P3: n = 7.

Clue 1: There is 2 and 7 in P1, but not in P2; there is 4 and 8 in P2, but not in P1, so Obid did not find any of those; he found either 3 or 6, which are choices for both P1 and P2.

Clue 2: There is 3 and 8 in P2, but not in P3; there is 5 and 7 in P3, but not in P2, so Zeb did not find any of those; he found either 4 or 6, which are choices for both P2 and P3.

Clue 3: On P3, McNeal isn't 4 or 5, J.D. isn't 4 or 7, and Obid isn't 6 or 7. Then McNeal is 7 (only one).

Clue 4: n = 6 (P1) isn't with n = 6 (P2). Obid had to answer 3 on both P1 and P2 [1].

Clue 5: n = 7 (P1) isn't with n = 7 (P3) who is McNeal, so McNeal didn't get 7 in P1.

Clue 6: n = 2 (P1) is with n = 8 (P2; only one that is ¼ of another answer). Zeb isn't 8 (P2), so didn't get 2 (P1).

Clue 7: The only boy you know is McNeal who got 7 for P3, which is correct. Then he also got 6 for P1 and 4 for P2 because one got all three answers correct; 6 (P1) is with 7 (P3) and 4 (P2); 7 (P3) is with 4 (P2).

Further Reasoning: J.D. is 2 (P1; only one) and 8 (P2) [6], which are 5 or 6 and not 4 on P3. Obid's answers (3, 3) don't go with 6 or 7 on P3. Zeb got 7 on P1 (only one) and 6 on P2 (only one), so he also got 6 on P3 [2]. J.D. got 5 on P3 (goes with 2 on P1 and 8 on P2) and Obid got 4 on P3 (goes with 3 on P1 and 3 on P2; only ones). n = 7 (P1) is with 6 (P3) and 6 (P2).

Answers: J.D., 2, 8, 5; McNeal, 6, 4, 7; Obid, 3, 3, 4; Zeb, 7, 6, 6.

Track and Field Day

Completed grid:

	long jump			
yards	4.89	5.14	5.25	5.39
inches	176	185	189	194
	discus throw			
yards	26.14	27.19	28.78	31.17
inches	941	979	1036	1122

Clue 1: Second and third place dash does not go with 81' 7" (979") throw; 16' 2" (194") jump; 979" (81' 7") does not go with 194" (16' 2").

Clue 2: Dellah did not place first or third in the dash.

Clue 3: Kendra did not place second in the dash; Kendra is not 1,036" (86' 4") throw; second place does not go with 1,036" (86' 4").

Clue 4: 5.25 yard (15' 9") jumper is not fourth in dash; she isn't first or second (Sigrid and 26.14 yard jumper are ahead of her), so she's third. Sigrid is not third or fourth; 26.14-yard

thrower (78' 5") is not third, fourth, or Sigrid; 15' 9" (third) jump is not Sigrid or 26.14-yard thrower (78' 5").

Clue 5: The 5.14-yard (15' 5") jumper is the 31.16-yard (93' 6") thrower; 15' 5" jump is not third, so 93' 6" throw is not third; 86' 4" throw is third (only one).

Further Reasoning: Dellah and Sigrid are not third, so they are not 86' 4" throw or 15' 9" jump. Aditi is 86' 4" throw, 15' 9" jump, and third-place dash. 16' 2" jump is 78' 5" throw and 14' 8" jump is 81' 7" throw (only ones). 16' 2" jump is not second [1], so 78' 5" throw is not second, it goes with first place, making 93' 6" throw connect with second-place dash and 81' 7" throw go with fourth place in dash (only ones). Therefore, 14' 8" is fourth in dash, 16' 2" is first, and 15' 5" is second. Sigrid did not throw 26.14 yards, so she did not place first. She placed second, Kendra placed first, and Dellah placed fourth (only ones). Using what you know about the corresponding distances and places, you can fill in the rest of the puzzle.

Answers: Aditi, 15' 9" jump, 86' 4" throw, third dash; Dellah, 14' 8" jump, 81' 7" throw, fourth dash; Kendra, 16' 2" jump, 78' 5" throw, first dash; Sigrid 15' 5" jump, 93' 6" throw, second dash.

Money for Music Lessons

Chart 1: rate per task: $25, $30, $15, $5, $20; times per task: 2, 1, 10, 2, 4.

Chart 2: rate per task: $5, $30, $25, $20, $15; times per task: 2, 1, 2, 4, 10.

Clue 1: Garage is x 2, paper route is x 10, so fill those in "times per task". Garage isn't $20 per task (so couldn't be $40 but there isn't a $40 total), isn't Alden, and isn't $5 per task (so isn't $10 total); $20 per task won't be Alden when you know how many times he requested and isn't paper route (there isn't a $200 total); Alden isn't paper route or $5 per task; paper route isn't $5 per task, so isn't $50. You can't mark much, but the information will be used later.

Clue 2: Garth isn't $25 per task; either Garth or $25 per task will be garage, which was 2 times [1]. Ralph will be 4x. Looking at the five uncles in Clue 1, Ralph must be $20 or $5 because he isn't garage (2x), paper route (10x), or Alden.

Clue 3: Alden is Goodwill, which is 1 time.

Clue 4: Paper route isn't $10 or $30, or $50 [1]; scooping isn't $10 or $150; pet care isn't $150 or $80. Pet sitting is 2x, so it is either Garth or $25 per time = $50. Ralph isn't pet sitting, so he's snow (only one).

Clue 5: Ralph isn't $30 or $10; Hugh isn't $150 or $10; Garth [pet care] isn't $150 or $80, or $50 because that would be $25 per task × 2 times, and Garth isn't $25 per task [2].

Pet care is $10 ($5 × 2 times) or $30 ($15 × 2 times). Looking back at Clue 1, the five uncles are garage, $20 per task, Alden, paper route, and $5 per task. Garth isn't garage, can't be $20 per task (no $40 total), isn't Alden, and isn't paper route, so he must be $5 per task × 2 = $10 for pet care. Fill in $5 "rate per task" and x 2 "times per task" above pet care and $10.

Further Reasoning: Garage must be $25 per task [2] since it is the other task done twice; fill in $25 above garage and fill in x 2 and $25 above $50; $50 isn't Ralph [4 times, Clue 2] or Alden [1 time, Goodwill, Clue 3]. Paper route is $150 (only one) so it is $15 rate per task, which isn't Alden, so Alden isn't $150.

Goodwill is $30 (only one), so Alden is $30. Fill $30 rate per task in above Goodwill; fill $30 rate per task and × 1 in above $30 total. Hugh isn't $150, so he isn't paper route. He is $50 (only one) and garage. Warren is paper route and $150 (only one).

Answers: Alden, Goodwill, $30; Garth, pet care, $10; Hugh, garage, $50; Ralph, scoop snow, $80; Warren, paper route, $150. Addison made $320, enough for 32 lessons.

Water, Water Everywhere

Chart: Week 1: 50 fl. oz., 55 fl. oz., 62 fl. oz., 67 fl. oz., 69 fl. oz.; Week 2: 6 ½ c., 7 ¼ c., 7 ⅝ c., 7 ⅞ c., 8 ¾ c.

Clue 1: 55 oz. W1 isn't with 8 ¾ c. W2.

Clue 2: Tamara isn't 6 ½ c. (W2), 67 oz (W1), Thursday, or Friday; 6 ½ c. isn't 67 oz., Monday, or Friday; 67 oz isn't Monday or Tuesday.

Clue 3: 62 oz. (W1) isn't Belle, 7 ⅝ c. (W2), Thursday, or Friday; Belle isn't 7 ⅝ c., Monday, or Friday; 7 ⅝ c. isn't Monday, Tuesday, Jolee, or Tamara (girls) because a boy drank 7 ⅝ oz.

Clue 4: Douglas is 50 oz. (W1).

Clue 5: 7 ⅞ is a girl, so it isn't Douglas, 50 oz. [Douglas, 4], Keegan, Jolee, or Friday; Douglas isn't Monday, and 50 oz. [4] isn't Monday; 7 ¼ c. isn't Tamara, 69 oz., or Friday; 69 oz. isn't Monday.

Clue 6: Jolee is Wednesday, Wednesday isn't 50 oz., 7 ⅝ c. [3], or 7 ⅞ c. [5].

Further Reasoning: Tamara isn't Wednesday [Jolee, 6], so 6 ½ c. can't be Thursday and 67 oz. can't be Friday [2]. Belle isn't Wednesday [Jolee, 6], so 62 oz. can't be Tuesday and 7 ⅝ c. can't be Thursday [3]; it's Friday (only one), but not 67 oz. [2]. Douglas isn't Wednesday [Jolee, 6], so 7 ⅞ can't be Tuesday [4]. 7 ⅞ isn't Jolee [5], so can't be Wednesday [Jolee, 6] and Douglas can't be Thursday. 7 ⅝ isn't Wednesday [girl (Jolee)], so Belle can't be Tuesday (so she's Thursday) and 62 oz. can't be Monday (so it's Wednesday). Belle isn't 50 oz. [4], so Thursday isn't 50 oz. and Thursday isn't 6 ½ c., so Belle isn't 6 ½ c. Wednesday is 62 oz., so Jolee [Wed., 6] is 62 oz., which isn't 7 ⅞ c. [5]. 67 oz. is Thursday (only one), so Belle is 67 oz. Then 6 ½ c. must be Wednesday [Jolee and 62 oz.] and Tamara must be Tuesday [2]. Then Keegan is Monday and Douglas is Friday (only ones). Because Douglas is Friday, 7 ⅞ c. is Thursday [5], Belle, and 67 oz.; 69 oz. is not Wednesday or Thursday, so 7 ¼ c. can't be Tuesday or Wednesday; it's Monday (only one), Keegan, and 55 oz. (only one); 7 ¼ c. is Monday; Keegan is 55 oz. and 7 ¼ c. Tuesday is 8 ¾ c. (only one); Tamara is 69 oz. (only one) and 8 ¾ c.; 69 oz. is 8 ¾ c. Friday is 50 oz. (only one); 7 ⅝ c. is 50 oz. (only one) and Douglas.

Answers: Belle, Thursday, 67 oz., 7 ⅞ c.; Douglas, Friday, 50 oz., 7 ⅝ c.; Jolee, Wednesday, 62 oz., 6 ½ c.; Keegan, Monday, 55 oz., 7 ¼ c.; Tamara, Tuesday, 69 oz., 8 ¾ c.

Totals: (Divide total ounces by 8). Belle had 130 oz. = 16.25 or 16 ¼ cups; Douglas had 111 oz. = 13.875 or 13 ⅞ cups; Jolee had 114 oz. = 14.25 or 14 ¼ cups; Keegan had 113 oz. = 14.125 or 14 ⅛ cups; Tamara had 139 oz. = 17.375 or 17 ⅜ cups, so Tamara drank the most water.

Down the Dogs

Clue 1: 3 pies isn't 3 dogs, 5 pies isn't 5 dogs, 6 pies isn't 6 hot dogs, 7 pies isn't 7 hot dogs, 8 pies isn't 8 hot dogs.

Clue 2: Manuel's team isn't 2 pies and Edgar's team isn't 8 pies.

Clue 3: Gerard and Liesa's teams are combinations of 2 pies + 7 hot dogs, 3 pies + 6 hot dogs, 5 pies + 4 hot dogs, or 6 pies + 3 hot dogs = 9 items, so they are not any of these: 7, 7 ½, or 8 pies; 5, 6 ½, or 8 hot dogs.

Clue 4: Suzy's team is not 2, 3, or 7 ½ pies and Adlai's team is not 6 ½, 7, or 8 hot dogs. Adlai's team is not 2, 3, or 7 ½ pies and Liesa's team is not 6 ½, 7, or 8 hot dogs.

Clue 5: 5 pieces of pie isn't with 3, 4, (5), or 6 ½ hot dogs and 7 pieces of pie isn't with 6, 6 ½, (7), or 8 hot dogs.

Clue 6: Adlai's team isn't 6 hot dogs (no 12 pies), 5 hot dogs (no 10 pies), 7 pies (no 3 ½ hot dogs), or 5 pies (no 2 ½ hot dogs), so he is 4 hot dogs and 8 pies or 3 hot dogs and 6 pies. Liesa's team isn't 5 hot dogs (no 2 ½ pies), 6 ½ (no 3 ¼ pies), 7 (no 3 ½ pies), 8 hot dogs (no 4 pies), 3 hot dogs (no 1 ½ pies), 5 pies (no 10 hot dogs), or 6 pies (no 12 hot dogs), so she is 2 pies and 4 hot dogs or 3 pies and 6 hot dogs.

Clue 7: Edgar, Gerard, and Manuel's teams didn't have 8 hot dogs; Jaylene, Liesa, and Suzy's teams didn't have 3 hot dogs.

Further Reasoning: In Clue 3, Liesa's team ate 9 items. From other clues, she didn't have 5 pies, so can't have 4 hot dogs, then she had 6 hot dogs (only one) and 3 pies = 9. In Clue 4, Adlai's team isn't 5 or 6 hot dogs [6], so Suzy's team can't be 7 or 8 pies. Liesa's team had 6 hot dogs, so Adlai's team had 8 pies, which goes with 4 hot dogs [6, half as many]. Then Suzy's team had 6 pies [4, two more]. In Clue 3, Gerard's team ate 9 items. It can't be 5 pies + 4 hot dogs (Adlai), and it can't be 3 hot dogs + 6 pies (Suzy), so his only other option is 2 pies + 7 hot dogs = 9. Then, 5 pies goes with 8 hot dogs (only one) and 7 pies must go with 5 hot dogs [5]. Edgar and Manuel's teams aren't 8 hot dogs, so they aren't 5 pies, Jaylene's team is 5 pies (only one) and 8 hot dogs. Suzy's team is 6 pies, which goes with 3 or 6 ½ hot dogs, but Suzy isn't 3 hot dogs [7], so her team is 6 ½ hot dogs. Then, 3 hot dogs goes with 7 ½ pies (only one). Look at Clue 2. Manuel must be 7 ½ pies (and 3 hot dogs) and Edgar is 7 pies (less, and 5 hot dogs).

Answers by team captains: Adlai, 8 pies, 4 hot dogs; Edgar, 7 pies, 5 hot dogs; Gerard, 2 pies, 7 hot dogs; Jaylene, 5 pies, 8 hot dogs; Liesa, 3 pies, 6 hot dogs; Manuel, 7 ½ pies, 3 hot dogs; Suzy, 6 pies, 6 ½ hot dogs.

The Pigskin

Teams are Atlanta Falcons, Chicago Bears, Denver Broncos, Miami Dolphins, and Minnesota Vikings.

Clue 1: Faith is Atlanta Falcons. Faith and Atlanta are not 6,267 or first; 6,267 is not fifth.

Clue 2: Simon is not 6,079 or 6,202 (5% of Roger), Miami Dolphins, fourth, or fifth; 6,079 is not first, fifth, or Miami Dolphins; Miami isn't first or second.

Clue 3: Mariah is third; she is not 6,205 so third isn't 6,205; she isn't Atlanta [Faith, 1] so third isn't Atlanta. Faith isn't third, so 6,267 can't be second [1]. Simon isn't third, so 6,079 can't be fourth and Miami can't be fifth [2].

Clue 4: Chicago Bears isn't 6,332 (3% of R).

Clue 5: Denver Broncos isn't fourth, fifth, Brock, or 6,205; Brock isn't first, fifth, or 6,205; 6,205 isn't first or second. Brock isn't third [Mariah, 3], so Denver can't be second and 6,205 can't be fourth. And, 6,205 is fifth (only one), so Brock can't be second (so he's fourth); Denver can't be first (so it's third, and Mariah).

Further Reasoning: Refer to Clue 1: Faith can't be fourth [Brock], so 6,267 can't be third [1]. Refer to Clue 2: Miami isn't third [Denver], it's fourth (only one); 6,079 can't be second (it's third, Denver and Mariah), and Simon can't be first (he's second); Porter is first and Faith is fifth (only ones). Because Faith is fifth, 6,267 is fourth [1] and Brock. Miami is fourth; Brock and 6,267 are fourth, so Miami is Brock and 6,267. Faith is Atlanta and fifth, 6,205 is fifth, so 6,205 is Faith and Atlanta. Porter is 6,202 and Simon is 6,332 (only ones); 6,202 is Chicago Bears and 6,332 is Minnesota Vikings (only ones), so Porter is Chicago, which is first and 6,202 is first. Simon (6,332) is Minnesota, which is second and 6,332 is second.

Answers: Brock, 6,267, Miami, fourth; Faith 6,205, Atlanta, fifth; Mariah, 6,079, Denver, third; Porter, 6,202, Chicago, first; Simon, 6,332, Minnesota, second.

Making the Grade

Note: There is no fourth grade and no fifth place.

Clue 1: Hellen is not sixth, seventh, or eighth place and Doyle is not first, second, or third place. There is no fifth place, so Doyle can't be eighth place because Hellen would be fifth place and Hellen can't be second place because Doyle would be fifth place. Hellen isn't first or second grade and she can't be sixth grade because there is no fourth grade. Betty isn't first or second place because someone placed at least two places higher.

Clue 2: Sixth grader is eighth place (which isn't Doyle or Hellen, so they aren't sixth grade).

Clue 3: Doyle isn't first grade or eighth grade (one lower than a girl); Lyle isn't eighth place (some girl placed one lower than Lyle).

Clue 4: Lyle isn't first, second, or third grades because he is three grades higher than someone, and he isn't seventh grade because there is no fourth grade; third place isn't eighth, seventh, or sixth [eighth place, 2] grades, and isn't first grade because there is no fourth grade (three grades ahead). Lyle isn't third place.

Clue 5: Rose isn't first grade and can't be fifth grade (no fourth). Doyle isn't last place (knew that already from Clue 1).

Clue 6: Alvin isn't eighth place and can't be fourth place (no fifth place); seventh grader isn't first place and can't be sixth place (no fifth place), and seventh grader isn't third place [4] (so Alvin isn't second place) and seventh grader isn't eighth place [2] (so Alvin isn't seventh place).

Clue 7: Second place is a girl, so it isn't Alvin, Doyle, or Lyle; second place isn't Betty or Hellen, so it's Rose or Virginia; seventh grader is one grade lower than second-place girl, so second place is eighth grade. Betty isn't first grade; Betty is one place lower than seventh grader who is either fourth place or seventh place, so Betty is fifth place or eighth place, but there is no fifth place, so Betty is eighth place, and the seventh grader is seventh place. Lyle isn't seventh grade, so he's not seventh

place. Alvin, Betty, and Hellen are not seventh place, so they are not seventh grade. Alvin, Betty, Doyle, Hellen, and Lyle are not second place, so they can't be eighth grade.

Clue 8: The sixth grader is eighth place, so the first grader is sixth place. Betty, Doyle, Hellen, Lyle, and Rose are not first grade, so they are not sixth place; it's Alvin or Virginia. Alvin is one place higher than seventh grader [6] who is seventh place, so Alvin is sixth place and first grade.

Further Reasoning: Betty was eighth place [and sixth grade, 2] and Alvin was sixth place, the one who got two places higher than Betty [1]. Hellen is two grades higher than Alvin [1, (1st grade)] so she is third grade. Doyle isn't sixth place so Hellen isn't third place [1]. From Clue 3, Doyle can't be second grade because first grade is a boy [Alvin] and he is a grade higher than a girl. Lyle can't be fourth place because there is no fifth place for a girl to be, so he is first place. Either Rose or Virginia must be the second-place girl [3]. Lyle is fifth or sixth grade, so first place is fifth or sixth grade, not second grade or third grade, but sixth grade isn't first place, it's eighth place, so fifth grade is first place and Lyle. He is three grades ahead of the one who got third place [4], so third place is with second grade. Then, fourth place is with third grade (only one), which is Hellen. Then, Doyle is seventh grade [1]. Because Doyle got seventh place, the child who got one place higher earned sixth place, and that's Alvin. Rose was one grade higher than Alvin who was the first grader, so Rose is second grade, which was third place, so Rose is third place. Then Virginia is second place. She is the one who earned one place lower than Lyle [3].

Answers: Alvin, first grade, sixth place; Betty, sixth grade, eighth place; Doyle, seventh grade, seventh place; Hellen, third grade, fourth place; Lyle, fifth grade, first place; Rose, second grade, third place; Virginia, eighth grade, second place.

How Many Hobbies?

Clue 1: Hampton is not Harley or Houston [boys, intro.]; hats is not Hadlee, Hayley, or Holly [girls, Intro.]; horses and hats are not Hampton (it's a girl). Horses (a girl) isn't Harley or Houston (boys). Horse girl has more than Hampton girl who has more than hat boy.

Clue 2: Hayley isn't Hazleton or harmonicas; Hazleton isn't harmonicas; harmonicas isn't Harley or Houston (boys). Hayley has more than Hazleton who has more than harmonica girl.

Clue 3: Holly isn't Hudson, hooded sweatshirts, or horses. Hooded sweatshirts isn't Hudson, Harley, or Houston (boys)—clue says *her* sweatshirt. Hudson isn't horses. You know hooded sweatshirts, harmonicas, and horses are all the girls' items, so none of the girls have hamsters or hats. Therefore, Holly collects harmonicas (only one).

Clue 4: Holly isn't Hazleton or Huxley; Hazleton isn't Harley or Houston (boys), so it is Hadlee (only one); Huxley isn't Hayley (g). Hadlee isn't hats, harmonicas, or hamsters, so Hazleton isn't hats, harmonicas, or hamsters. Holly isn't Hudson or Huxley, so harmonicas isn't Hudson or Huxley. Huxley isn't horses [girl, 1] or sweatshirts [girl, 3]. The only items for Hudson and Huxley are hamsters and hats (harmonicas, horses, and hooded sweatshirts are eliminated), so they are boy towns. No girls are from Hudson or Huxley. Hampton, Hazleton, and Hiawatha are girl towns (not Harley or Houston) with horses, harmonicas, and hooded sweatshirts, not hats or hamsters. Hazleton girl (Hadlee) has more than Holly who has more than Huxley boy.

Clue 5: Hiawatha isn't Houston or horses; Houston isn't horses [girl, 1]. Combine Clues 1 and 5 to determine most to least: Hiawatha, Houston, horses, Hampton, hats.

Further Reasoning: Girl order is Hiawatha, horses, Hampton, so Hayley must be Hiawatha (more than Hazleton girl [4] and harmonica girl [2]); horses must be Hadlee [Hazleton] and Hampton must be Holly [harmonicas]. Then Hayley collects hooded sweatshirts (the other girl hobby). Boy order is Houston, then hats, so Houston is not hats, Harley is; Houston is hamsters. Combining Clues 4 and 5, you know that Houston has more items than the girl who collects horse figurines [5 (Hadlee who is from Hazleton)] who has more than Holly and Huxley boy [4], so Houston can't be Huxley; he is Hudson and Harley is Huxley. So, Hudson is hamsters and Huxley is hats.

Answers: Hadlee, Hazleton, horses; Harley, Huxley, hats; Hayley, Hiawatha, hooded sweatshirts; Holly, Hampton, harmonicas; Houston, Hudson, hamsters.

To determine the order of most to least:

Clue 1: Horse girl has more than Hampton girl who has more than hat boy.

Clue 2: Hayley has more than Hazleton who has more than harmonica girl.

Clue 4: Hazleton girl (Hadlee) has more than Holly who has more than Huxley boy.

Clue 5: Hiawatha has more than Houston who has more than horses [followed by Hampton, then hats, 1], so order must be: Hiawatha, Houston, horses, Hampton, hats. In order from most to least: Hayley, Houston, Hadlee, Holly, Harley.

Gallons for Gals

Cups: 64, 112, 192, 224, 336, 384, 448.
Quarts: 16, 28, 48, 56, 84, 96, 112.
Gallons: 4, 7, 12, 14, 21, 24, 28.

Clue 1: The only combinations are for horses to be 192 c. and lemonade to be 64 c. and for horses to be 336 c. with lemonade 112 c. Save this information for later.

Clue 2: Leanne used either 14, 24, or 28 gallons of water. You can save for later that she did not make food, gas the boat, or wash dishes.

Clue 3: 64, 112, 192, and 224 all are multiples of other numbers. Velvet could have used any of these amounts to make potato salad.

Clue 4: Natalie used either 56, 96, or 112 quarts. Gigi used either 28, 48, or 56 quarts.

Clue 5: D'Andra used 7, 14, 21, or 28 gallons. Quasondra used 12 or 24 gallons.

Clue 6: You know Velvet made potato salad and Gigi made lemonade. Try the options: 7 (Gigi) × 4 (Velvet) = 28 gallons (OK), 12 (G) × 4 (V) = 48 gallons (too much). All other combinations will be too high. Velvet used 4 gallons to make potato salad and Gigi used 7 gallons for lemonade.

Further Reasoning: Natalie used 14 gallons [4] to clean latrines. 28 gallons was used to fill the boat with gas. Leanne did not gas the boat [2], neither did Quasondra or D'Andra [5]. Yvonne filled the boat. Leanne used 24 gallons, Quasondra used 12 gallons, and D'Andra used 21 gallons (only ones). D'Andra watered the horses [1]. Leanne didn't do dishes [2], so she had to have done laundry. Quasondra did dishes (only one).

Answers: D'Andra, 21 gallons, horses; Gigi, 7 gallons, lemonade; Leanne, 24 gallons, laundry; Natalie, 14 gallons, latrine; Quasondra, 12 gallons, water for dishes; Velvet, 4 gallons, potato salad; Yvonne, 28 gallons, boat gas.

About the Author

Marilynn L. Rapp Buxton currently teaches the fourth-, fifth-, and sixth-grade talented and gifted program at Waverly-Shell Rock Community Schools in Waverly and Shell Rock, IA. She also teaches a self-designed curriculum of creative and critical thinking skills in classrooms, math enrichment for high-ability students, is the elementary school yearbook editor, and coaches Future Problem Solving teams. She received a bachelor's degree from Iowa State University and has taken numerous graduate courses through Drake University, University of Iowa, University of Northern Iowa, Viterbo University, and Marycrest College for her K–12 gifted endorsement and educational certifications.

Her curriculum ideas and student projects have been published as "Teacher Features" in *Iowa Talented and Gifted Magazine.* She also is the author of *Math Logic Mysteries* published by Prufrock Press. She has enjoyed presenting at the Iowa Talented and Gifted Conference, Wisconsin Talented and Gifted Conference, Midwest Regional Middle Level Conference, area gifted and talented forums, and local staff in-services. She enjoys spending time with family, swimming, singing in Sweet Adelines International and church choir, and doing Sudoku and matrix logic puzzles.